WHEN LIFE HURTS
Healing Themes from the Gospels

WHEN LIFE HURTS:
Healing Themes From the Gospels

Andrew M. Greeley

THE THOMAS MORE PRESS
Chicago, Illinois

These meditations, in somewhat different form, have appeared in **Markings,** a newsletter published by the Thomas More Association.

ISBN: 0-88347-220-1

Contents

Can there be life without worry?   9

God's transforming love   12

No need to pretend   15

When we share a meal   19

The peril of indecision   23

God's love for us   26

Searching for treasure   29

Paralyzed with fear   32

We won't be quitters   36

Settling our quarrels   40

Being truly sorry   43

Can you be too generous?   47

Not honoring a promise   51

Loneliness, isolation, alienation   54

Are permanent commitments obsolete?   58

The gift of healing   62

Growing up   65

The implications of friendship   68

Why do we envy success   72

Sometimes it takes courage   75

The real "bad" language   79

Teenagers versus parents   83

Are you satisfied with your life?   87

Old age is not for sissies   91

The old order is always changing   94

Two kinds of sorrow   98

Are we prepared to talk about it?   102

Too weary to care   106

A question of love   109

Searching for security   113

A friend no matter what   117

Being in love is hard work   121

Boring, boring, boring   124

The pain of ingratitude   127

But they are not like us   131

Trying too hard   135

Yearning for a home   139

So much to do, so little time   143

Hanging by a thread   147

Humility is not self-deprecation   150

Standing by your friends   154

Learning to love one another   157

Our ingratitude to God   161

Who said marriage was easy?   165

Resisting temptation   169

The ultimate bad news   173

A challenging invitation   178

While most of the Gospel stories these re-flections are based on will be familiar to a majority of readers, the scripture citations are given at the end of each section for the benefit of those who would like to refresh their memories.

Can there be life without worry?

JUST as the robin or the first crocus is a sign of spring, just as the melting snow suggests that budding trees cannot be too far off, so there are signs and portents in the personalities of each of us that life is going to be all right. Two such moments of confidence are reconciliations after quarrels and tenderly caring for someone you love. For during the quarrel and the sullen silence afterwards, you wonder whether perhaps the love was all a mistake. But when the floodgates of reconciliation are open, we know that it was not a mistake. Similarly, it is a marvelously reassuring experience to be tenderly cared for by someone who loves us. It is even more reassuring to be able to give another tender care and see grateful acceptance. To console, to care for, to minister to a loved one is an experience which ignites confidence as few things in the human condition can.

The words in the Sermon on the Mount are some of the most beautiful that have ever been written. They reveal Jesus as a poetic and visionary person who knew exactly how to touch the most vulnerable aspect of the human personality, the most eager, intimate corner of the human heart. We are told simply and caressingly that there is nothing to worry about, that everything will be all right, that God will care for us and protect us, that we will be forgiven, that it is all right to trust, all right to hope, all right to relax and not worry. It is very good news indeed, even though most of the time most of us live as though we can scarcely believe it is true. It is instructive to imagine how we would live if we were not afraid, if we were not prey to anxiety, worry, and concern, if we could, as John Shea has suggested in a lovely poem, "worry the Kingdom into life instead of ourselves to death."

The thought of a life without worry is extraordinarily appealing—kind of like an endless vacation, indeed, an endless vacation in a warm, sunny climate when our normal place of residence is cold and covered with a thick blanket of snow. Life without worry is very like a permanent winter vacation in the sunlight. It would be so, so nice. It is not possible, of course, because what would happen if we stopped worrying? God protect us from all the harm that would occur if we stopped worrying about it. So, despite Jesus, we know that worry is effective. It does fend off catastrophe, it does prevent disaster from happening, and it may even permit us to add a centimeter or so to our height.

It is pretty difficult to remember when we started worrying for the first time, when anxiety became as necessary in our life as breathing. But it is quite easy to remember the last time we worried. Was it a minute ago? Five minutes, ten minutes, or even as far back as just before we came into church? The distance between the theory preached by Jesus in the gospel and the practice of our daily lives is staggering, enormous, overwhelming, indescribable. But Jesus tells us the heavenly Father loves us, that he will take care of us and protect us even more than the birds and the flowers. Jesus clearly does not mean a strict comparison between our fate and the fate of the flowers or the birds; he means that the massive, profligate gift of life which covers the earth is so wonderful, so awesome, so colorful, so beautiful, so warm, and so dazzling, that only with great effort can we disbelieve in a loving, protecting, motherly Giver of Life.

As in virtually everything he says, Jesus touches instincts deep within the human personality, reinforces, validates, strengthens, calls from us that which we would dearly like to believe is true and that which in our best moments we do believe is true. He tells us that such instincts are not self-deception but rather revelation. On a spring day, with the birds singing, the flowers blooming, we know that there is Goodness. Jesus tells us that we are right; his heavenly Father's loving goodness is warmer, more spectacular, more generous, more gracious than we in our wildest moments can imagine. When we hear the words of the gospel, one part of us is tempted to respond, "Oh, if only that were true!" and another part to answer, "I knew it was true all along!"

(Matthew 6:24-34)

God's transforming love

WHEN Jesus was transfigured on Mount Tabor, an absent God did not suddenly become present. Rather, a God who was present was seen briefly, transiently (but overwhelmingly) more clearly than he had been seen before. There are times in life when God seems to be absent, but when he reveals himself, as he did on Tabor, the experience is not of an absent God returning but of an always present and loving God disclosing himself again. We exist in a protective envelope, in a loving caress, in a fond embrace which is so much a part of our existence that we are often not aware of it. It must disclose itself in special ways in order that we may become aware once more of how tender it is, how powerful it is, and how it is always present.

So the purpose of the transfiguration was to reveal the presence of God's loving goodness to the apostles through Jesus and in a special way to prepare them for the difficulties, the suffering, the dangers, and the heartaches that lay ahead as they went up to Jerusalem. We, too, are often transformed in the course of our lives—but not so dramatically—by experiences of the presence of God, or at least experiences of the presence of a loving, caressing goodness which reveals itself to us sometimes spectacularly, more often gently and subtly, as caring for us, tending us, caressing us, holding us in the palm of its hands. Often we are so busy, so distracted, so worn by monotony and routine that we are barely aware of these intimations of grace which in truth bombard us every day of our life with spectacular sunbursts of God's love. The secret of having our own "Tabor experiences" often in our life is to train ourselves to be ready for them, to listen to them, to recognize them when they come to us. For they are light in darkness, hope in sorrow, joy in sadness, and rejuvenating love in weariness.

The great Catholic thinker and visionary, Karl Rahner, compares God's presence to light. We only notice the light when it goes out; otherwise, it is a given, a constant, something to be assumed, something to be taken for granted, something which is as natural to us as getting up in the morning, eating our meals, washing our hands and face, breathing. But since light is a given, we rarely examine it, pay attention to it, reflect upon it. Similarly, Rahner says, God's presence as revealed in our daily experiences of grace, of renewed hope and courage, joy and love, faith and conviction, of a smiling face, a contagious laugh, a forgiving touch, a dazzling embrace, is so much a part of our ordinary existence that we rarely stop to think what such experiences reveal to us about the meaning of our life and about the God who discloses himself to us through these very ordinary, yet extraordinary, interludes of grace.

God will transform us if we permit him to—not so spectacularly as he transformed Jesus on Tabor, perhaps, but in the same way and in the same direction. We must, however, be open, sensitive, ready for transformation. We must permit ourselves the leisure, the time, the luxury, to enjoy, to revel in, to be illumined by, and to be delighted with the endless brickbats of goodness which bounce off us in our daily life. Humanlike, we focus on the troubles, the misfortunes, the sorrows, the problems and miss the transforming goodness which swirls around us, baiting us constantly, renewing us, blessing us, encouraging us, loving us. Such caressing goodness does not promise that we will not have to go up to Jerusalem, that we will not have to suffer our own Via Dolorosa and crucifixion; it does not guarantee us that we will be spared the ultimate disaster of death. The caressing goodness which is God's transforming love enveloping us merely tells us that God continues to love us no matter what happens, and therefore we should lift up our eyes, take heart, and continue to live.

(Matthew 17:1-19)

No need to pretend

THINK about the close friends you have had during your life: the toddler you played with before you went to school, friends at the various stages of grammar school, the clique you hung out with in high school, your college confidants, the people you are most likely to socialize with now, the friend it is a pleasure to visit, those you turn to for advice, reassurance, comfort when you need it. Generally speaking, few of us maintain continuity in friendships throughout the various stages in the life cycle. Our preschool playmates are rarely our closest friends in adulthood—though some people do maintain close relationships with people they have known since first grade. Yet a single factor probably runs through all the relationships you could award the honored title "friendship." It is the nature of friendship that we are able to relax with a friend, to let down our hair, to be ourselves, to drop our defenses, to abandon our pretenses. A friend is not a person to whom, despite the novel *Love Story,* you never have to say you're sorry. A friend is rather somebody with whom we don't have to pretend.

Friendship, as defined above, is not an easy relationship to develop. To abandon pretense, to throw away our defenses requires a considerable amount of courage. We have to be confident that the other will not hurt us. Most human friendships are in fact only relationships of frequent interactions with most of the pretense still maintained. People have to know one another well before they feel safe about dropping their pretenses.

Even in marriage, friendship may be a long time in coming. The engaged couple, the bride and groom, the newlywed, even the mature husband and wife frequently keep up defenses, pretensions, phoniness, fakery. It is not exaggeration to say that only when a marriage also becomes a friendship will it become happy and durable. One can well judge the quality of one's marital relationship by measuring the amount of phoniness and pretense that remains in it.

In the gospel Jesus prays for his "band of brothers," his "happy few," as though they were friends. He has called them not servants but friends. He feels utterly at ease in being himself with and for them, and they respond the same way in their reactions to him. They must have learned early in the game that there was no point in pretending with Jesus, because he saw through pretenses anyway. He loved them not for what they pretended to be but for who in fact they were.

We have heard so many times the affectionate farewell discourse of Jesus to his apostles in the Sundays after Easter that it doesn't make all that much impression on us. Okay, he called them friends not servants, and he spoke to them and prayed over them because he loved them and there were no pretenses, no phoniness, no barriers in his relationship to them. We do not realize, however, the shattering implications of such friendship with Jesus not only for his immediate followers but for those of us who come after them who have the same promise of friendship. For it is reassuring to know that Jesus loves us despite the fact that he sees through our pretenses, and that in our relationship to him pretense is neither possible nor necessary. It is a terrifying challenge.

For if we are the friends of Jesus, if we are good enough to be loved by him even though he sees through all of our pretenses, then it may possibly be that we are good enough to be loved by others who also, more or less, see through our fakery. There is a kind of comic dimension to human relationships. Two people who are friends really do see the pretense and love the other person (despite the pretense) for who the person is. Nonetheless, the barriers are not dropped, the dance of pretense continues, and the fiction is maintained that it is the phony self that is loved and not the real self. And what is that real self that is truly loved? Another level of the comedy of the human condition is that the self that is truly loved is the self we would like to show but are afraid to so we try to cover it up and protect it by pretension. We are loved for who we are, and who we are is usually who we want to be; but it is the one we want to be that we pretend not to be for fear of our inadequacy of living up to such a self-image. It sounds complicated, but in moments of honesty between close friends, especially between husbands and wives who are also friends, it quickly becomes apparent that the fakery doesn't work and that the real self is known and adored far more than the fake self.

The conclusion we should come to from the fact that we are the friends of Jesus, and run all the risks of being others' friends, is not that we be reckless or uncalculating or undiscriminating in our friendships. The wise person gives his or her total self to very few people. He

17

or she does give it to some people despite the terrors involved in such a gift. One of the reasons for giving oneself so generously is that Jesus has already given himself to us.

(John 17:1-11)

When we share a meal

A HUSBAND and wife are in the midst of a quarrel, one that has been building up for weeks, perhaps even for months or years. They are, however, scheduled to go out to dinner with another couple. The customs of our society being what they are, it is necessary to pretend that no conflict exists. So the man and woman go through the motions of a relaxed, pleasant, fun-filled evening, even though they are inwardly boiling at one another and frustrated by the need to pretend. They are acting out, in other words, a ritual of love when the love between them is dormant at least.

Such situations—and they happen in all marriages and in many friendships—demonstrate that sharing a meal is an act of intimacy. We incorporate food into our body together with somebody else while at the same time we are, as it were, incorporating that other person into our personality as a friend, companion, partner, one who is intimate to us in our life. There are varying degrees of intimacy, depending upon the partner and the meal. The sharing of the food, however, and the sharing of the personality are closely linked phenomena. Just as we want to share food with those with whom we are intimate, so we tend to be intimate with those with whom we share food. Such things are not absolutely necessary, of course, but they represent strong propensities and inclinations of our personality. They are the ordinary, the commonplace way of doing things.

So it was not accidental that Jesus directed that the

Eucharist be the memory of his presence among us and that he represents himself to us in the Eucharist. The Eucharist is a banquet, it is a ritual which re-enacts, reaffirms, and revalidates our incorporation into the body of those who are the friends of Jesus, that group who by consuming the Word of God and by consuming the Eucharist are united in loving intimacy with Jesus, with one another, and with the Father in heaven.

The love we celebrate and reinforce in the Eucharist, however, is not easy. No love is ever easy, because the attractive, repellant powers involved in love are so powerful. We are drawn to one another and we are afraid of one another. We want to give ourselves, but we fear being hurt; we want to be united with the other, yet the other terrifies us. We want the ecstasy that comes from union, but we do not want to pay the price of surrender. We want to run toward the other, but when we get close we want to flee. We want to incorporate the other and be incorporated by the other; we are terrified, though, that we will lose our identity by such an act. So we compromise, not giving ourselves over to complete love but also not retreating into hate. The name of the compromise is ambivalence, a mixture of love and hate, with love being just a little bit stronger, keeping the intimacy from breaking apart. It characterizes our marital loves, our close friendships, relationships between parents and children, and relationships with our fellow Christians and with God.

We eat our common meals together, whether they be at church or at home, harboring our petty resentments and our intense affections, but trying to keep everything low key, casual, relaxed; we try to "cool it" with one another and with God because that way we're safe. It protects us from the roller coaster of up-and-down emotion which is inevitable when we permit love the freedom to flourish. We don't unincorporate ourselves, but we don't incorporate ourselves either; we don't withdraw from our communities, but we don't commit ourselves intensely to them. Being afraid of both heaven and hell, in other words, we search for limbo. We eat the bread of eternal life but cool our consumption down to an empty Sunday morning or Saturday evening ritual. There are no implications for the rest of our lives. Not wanting to be hot or cold, we are lukewarm, and we try to forget that Jesus said he would vomit the lukewarm out of his mouth.

To love someone else is a risk. The only true lover is a gambler, sometimes a reckless one. It matters not whether we love God or another human being. To act out the ritual which we celebrate in the Eucharist or at an intimate meal is to put ourselves on the line, to risk everything on a single throw of the dice, to "go for broke" with our personality. The potential payoff is great, but so are the potential losses. If there is no touch of the reckless gambler, the "go-for-broke" risk-taker in our personalities, we will never give ourselves in love and never trust the gift of love from someone else. Then we will settle for the every day routine of going to work, cleaning the house, cooking the meal, putting the children to bed, watching television, going to mass on Saturday or Sunday, convinced that this is what life is really all about, closing our ears to the promises of the gospel and to the challenge implied in every Eucharistic banquet, the challenge of risk-taking and gambling,

21

and the reckless search for love. Such is a safe life, but it is a life in which the yearnings of the human heart, the anguish of the human soul, the desperate hunger of the human personality are stifled because they suggest danger and possible defeat.

If we really believed the Eucharist was the bread of eternal life and that when we ate it we were guaranteed through our union with God and Jesus that we would be risen up on the last day, then we would not be afraid to risk ourselves in human love. Our human loves are weak, mediocre, compromising, superficial, routine things when we don't trust the divine love which has been offered to us.

(John 6:51-59)

The peril of indecision

PICTURE yourself in an auto showroom. Somebody has just given you a blank check to buy a new car. On one side of you is a Mercedes 250 SL and on the other side a Porsche 900. The speedy sportscar or the luxurious sedan? The sex symbol or the symbol of affluence? The car that says you're a live wire or the car that says here's success? You can only have one; you vacillate back and forth, and the time for your choice runs out. Which one will you pick? Which way will you go? Which of these prized objects will you choose?

He who hesitates, they say, is lost. If you don't choose between your Mercedes and your Porsche, somebody else may come along and take both. Similarly, a young man finds himself in the utterly delightful position of having two beautiful and charming women in love with him and being quite unable to choose between such wonderful potential mates. If he hesitates too long, they are both likely to tire of him and he will be faced with the appalling lack of choice. You cannot hesitate forever; you cannot waffle, shilly-shally, vacillate, hesitate, procrastinate, indefinitely. There is a time dimension in human life, so that if one does not exercise one's options with some degree of promptness, the options may be lost irrevocably.

Sometimes indecisiveness is merely a pretext for not deciding and staying with the status quo. A man who must choose between a job he already has and a new, potentially more interesting job hesitates, procrastinates, dilly dallies until the new job is gone. In effect, he makes a choice but does not admit it to himself. However, there is also the possibility that while he agonizes over his choice he so neglects the job he has that that job slips away too. "Time," as the old newsreels used to say, "marches on," and he who hesitates may find opportunities slipping through his fingers like melting snowflakes.

Jesus urges decisiveness upon his followers. You must choose either for Jesus or against him. You must finally believe his Good News or reject it. You must accept his vision of a love-animated universe or turn your back on it. There is time, though less time than there was and less time than we imagine there still might be. Eventually, however, we will run out of time, and Jesus reminds us with the passionate urgency that marked everything he did not to delay our choice too long. Because then we might lose everything. The gospel does not attack family life or family loyalties, except when they are used as excuses not to choose for Jesus. To make his point clearer, to hammer it home, Jesus says, I don't want to hear any excuses, not even the most personal and most poignant of excuses. Get with it while there is yet time, because if you don't, then you will lose an incredible opportunity.

Indecisiveness, vacillation, hesitancy are especially deadly when the issue is love. If we hesitate too long to make our commitment of love, to celebrate it with our loved one, or to enjoy the pleasures of love, then there may be no more opportunities. Parents die eventually and we can't tell them any more how much they mean to us. No one can look back over an intense love relationship and be perfectly content with his or her contribution. So many easy opportunities to express love have been wasted because of timidity, suspicion, fear, defensiveness. The poignancy of lost opportunities is especially haunting when we realize that as a season comes to an end, so one more season of love has passed and one more set of opportunities in our life have been lost. As has been said so many times, human love and divine love reflect and mirror one another. If you have the courage to seize the present moment in human love, you will do the same in responding to the invitation of Jesus. He who bravely and confidently seizes Jesus' message of God's love for us will also seize the opportunities that exist in human love relationships. In fact, the essence of Jesus' message in the gospel today is not anti-family, it is pro-family, because it urges us to be decisive in all our loves and it guarantees the safety of such decisiveness that is to be found in believing as fully and as truly as we can that God loves us.

(Matthew 10:37-42)

JESUS promises rest to "all who labor and are overburdened." But what does he mean? Who isn't overburdened? Who doesn't need rest? Certainly he did not find much peace or rest in this life and very few of his followers—at least his dedicated followers—have found rest either. Bali Hai, the magical tropical island, is always just over the horizon. Next year we'll have a real vacation, but this year there are too many things to do, too many things to worry about, too many reasons for getting back as quickly as we can. The blessed leisure that Jesus promised seems like an illusion.

Mind you, much of the stewing and fretting, the hustling and rushing, the worry and the anxiety, the endless looking at the watch—as though by doing that we could slow the pace of time—is unnecessary. If we had more faith, perhaps we could give up such frantic activity, perhaps we could go away on a summer vacation and relax. Even if it weren't a trip to Bali Hai, it could be a time of modest refreshment. All right, if that's what Jesus meant, fair enough. If we had greater faith, we would relax more, not be so weary and tired, and would feel refreshed more often. We would come home from vacation at least in a little better spirits than when we left. But is that all Jesus meant? The promise of peace and rest, of refreshment and relaxation in the gospel somehow seems to apply to more than just the quiet that comes from worrying less.

The "something extra" that seems to be involved in the gospel has perhaps more to do with love than with faith. It is not so much the love we have for God as the love that God has for us. A yoke is a harness borne by two beasts of burden. Jesus is telling us that he is yoked with us, harnessed with us, in bearing the burdens of our life. The peace and refreshment he promises us is a direct result of that sharing of the burdens. When a man and woman who deeply love one another bear the burden of life together, the physical weight of such burdens may not decline; the problems are as serious, the difficulties as threatening, the uncertainties as perplexing as if each carried a separate burden. Yet, precisely because they are doing it together in an atmosphere and climate of love, psychologically the burdens are lightened, for the intensity, the joy, the pleasure of their love make the burdens seem less heavy and the effort less wearying. Jesus tells us in the gospel that we are caught up in a love affair with him and with the heavenly father; and the intensity of that love—if we permit ourselves to experience and appreciate it—provides the peace, the rest, the relaxation, the renewal we need to continue. Physically we may be exhausted; psychologically, however, we have hidden reservoirs of strength precisely because we realize that we are loved.

All too often the love of God is discussed as though it were an obligation imposed on us. We are obliged to love God. In fact, it is the other way around. God is the one who is obliged to love us because he has committed himself to that love. Ours is the privilege of accepting his invitation. Nor is this merely a metaphor or poetry. The universe is animated by love, and we are the target of that love, even if at times there are things that happen to us that don't seem to be compatible with love.

27

Andrew M. Greeley

God tries to communicate with us about his love for us every day in a thousand ways—the blue sky, the stars, the cooling rain, the fluffy white clouds, the touch of a loving hand, a friendly smile, a warm embrace at the end of the day are all revelations of God's love and occasion the psychological peace and rest promised to us in the gospel. If we are not able to relax and enjoy ourselves on our vacation, the reason probably is that we have not learned how to relax and enjoy ourselves in the ordinary moments of peace and joy which are available despite the burdens, the difficulties, and the hardships of our daily lives.

(Matthew 11:25-30)

Searching for treasure

OCCASIONALLY we read in the newspaper about someone who has discovered a priceless heirloom in an attic or an original Rembrandt in the basement of an art store or a rare book that has somehow slipped behind the bookshelf. We are astonished at the good fortune of someone who has stumbled by chance on an object of enormous value. In the gospel Jesus presents for us the picture of the hardworking day laborer or the equally hardworking traveling merchant who by chance discovers an object of enormous value, one which will quite literally transform his life. Jesus invites us to picture the excitement, the energy, the enthusiasm which the fortunate one throws into his efforts to make his own ticket to a better life.

From Robert Louis Stevenson's *Treasure Island* of long ago to Nick Nolte and Jacqueline Bisset in *The Deep* the search for buried treasure has had an obsessive fascination for most of us. The characters of Ben Gunn and Long John Silver were and still are favorites of children. The attraction of buried treasure is precisely what Jesus, with his remarkable insight into human psychology, depicts in the gospel: enormous good fortune and the promise of enormous fortune—a happy change which opens up the opportunity of a very happy life. We cannot imagine Mr. Nolte and Ms. Bisset turning their backs on the buried treasure beneath them. And if Long John Silver and his magic parrot should give up their hunt for treasure, we would be terribly disappointed in them. Only a fool would pass up an opportunity like that, we tell ourselves. Sure, there's suffering and pain, sure, there's some sacrifice in the pursuit of buried treasure, but when you know the treasure is there and almost within your grasp, how could you possibly give up and turn away? That's precisely the point Jesus is making in the parable.

It is not a parable that requires all that much explanation or interpretation. The point is all too clear: the gospel that Jesus came to preach, the story about his Father in heaven and his Father's love that he came to tell, the opportunity he provides are buried treasure. Only the coward, the nitwit, the incompetent, the dullard, the fool would turn away from the possibilities that Jesus offers. How can it be that the pearl of great price, the buried treasure in the field, the gold in the sunken Spanish galleon are pursued vigorously and the opportunity that Jesus provides with the story of God's love is pursued lackadaisically if at all? Obviously, the Good News of Christianity does not look like buried treasure or hidden gold to many of us. We may claim that it does, but in fact we can take this particular pearl of great price or leave it alone—and mostly we leave it alone.

Treasure-hunting novels are enormously popular. The story of buried treasure has lost none of its appeal since the day of Jesus. The problem for us today is rather to believe that the truth revealed to us by Jesus, that the God disclosed to us through Jesus' words and deeds does indeed represent something at least as valuable as buried gold, a misplaced Rembrandt, or a jewel of fabulous worth. We have heard the parable so often, we take it so much for granted, that it really doesn't hit us the way it ought to. We can't quite accept the fact that the knowledge of God's love should transform our lives every bit as much as the buried treasure transforms the life of the day laborer. We can understand such things as wealth, power, and leisure; we can realize that they do transform the life of the one who acquires them; but we can't quite comprehend how the same thing happens to us when we accept the message of Jesus. Wealth, leisure, and power mitigate if they do not eliminate such things as fear, anxiety, worry, uncertainty, the harshness of our daily struggle. Jesus is telling us quite definitely in today's parable that accepting his vision of God will accomplish the same thing for us—indeed would accomplish it more effectively and more decisively than would the treasure in the field or the Rembrandt in the basement. We find that very hard to believe. We agree when we hear the parable of the buried treasure, as we have through all the years since we first heard it. But still we do not take it seriously; we do not believe that our life is an adventure, and that the buried treasure which ought to give power, energy, and drive to our life is a treasure that is ours for the asking when we realize how much God loves us.

(Matthew 13:44-52)

31

Paralyzed with fear

SOME people "panic" more often than others. Some of us are panic prone; we become flustered, befuddled, spaced out, tied up in knots with relatively little provocation. But such moments of panic do not compare with the real terror that comes when, for example, we see a car heading for us and we are pretty certain there will be an accident; or when the elevator grinds to a halt and sways perilously somewhere between floors; or when the ladder begins to tip; or when the man with a knife or a gun demands our money. In such moments of pure fright, we understand how Peter felt when the winds and the waters of the Sea of Galilee began to swirl around him. We have no trouble at all understanding his cry, "Save me, Lord, I perish!" We know the feeling.

When Jesus calmed the waters that terrified his disciples he tells us again that God will really take care of us, that there are no grounds for our terror. We should note the subtle psychology of this important incident. Peter and the other disciples have already witnessed the miracle of the loaves and the fishes. Scarcely an hour or two later they are out on the lake in a storm. Somehow they cannot persuade themselves that the Jesus who fed so many people will be able to protect them in the storm. It is easy to poke fun at the followers of Jesus. At times they were pretty funny people. But they are everyperson, and we are exactly like them. No matter how many times God has protected us, no matter how many times we have been touched by grace, no matter how many good things have happened to us in our life, we are still skeptical cynics, still easily terrified by the worries and the anxieties and the fears of life, still incapable of even modest bravery in the face of difficulty and trial.

Obviously confidence in God will not prevent terror when we see the mugger's knife or the out-of-control car bearing down on us. Cool nerves under such circumstances are partly a matter of genes, partly a matter of life experience, and, perhaps, also partly a matter of how routine and habitual is our confidence in God's love. However, the important issue is not the cool hand and steady nerve in moments of instantaneous, unexpected crisis. Rather the important question is whether we panic in terror in sustained crises, whether they be a terrible conflict in the family; a major problem in our work environment; a frightening exam, paper, or dissertation; a tragic illness; a tragic loss of someone we love. The instant impact of such fear-full events is paralysis. But how do we bounce back from such paralysis? How long before we realize, like Peter did, that Jesus is extending his hand to help us?

It is human to be paralyzed momentarily, and the time of the moment may last several days. But without faith in God's love and in the message that Jesus can help us, we are in trouble. Blind unreasoning terror which paralyzes our every action is ultimately the most fearful thing in human life, because it prevents us from mobilizing our resources, our ingenuities, our skills, our faith. If we have experienced long-term interludes of paralysis caused by fears, we should ask ourselves why our faith seems so weak. The question need not be asked out of a sense of failure or guilt, for, after all, Peter, the head of the apostles, gave us an excellent example of how no one has any right to presume that faith is strong enough and no one has any right to give up in guilt when faith hasn't been strong enough. All weakness proves is that we are weak. But it should also force us to ask the question of why we are weak.

And even if we have not been through such interludes when terror threatens to paralyze us for a substantial period of time, we ought to take a good hard look at how much power fear has in our life, how much it dominates and controls our actions and attitudes. For if we are fearful, frightened, quaking people when there are no terrible or serious things threatening us, then there is no reason to think that we will turn into paragons of strength and courage and fidelity when we get bombed with the Big Problem.

The difficulty for Peter was not that he was afraid. (Who wouldn't be afraid, walking on waters with the wind and the waves trying to pull you down?) Peter's problem, and our problem, is that fear which could well have released the energies and the dynamism he needed to build up his confidence, instead caused him to lose his calm. The challenge for Peter, and for all of us, is not to avoid fear; that we cannot do. It is rather to keep calm despite our fear. Jesus did not promise us an easy, unthreatening, unterrifying, smooth, placid, untroubled life. He didn't tell Peter that the wind and the waves wouldn't be scary; he merely told him, in effect, that if he trusted in God's love, the scariness of the wind and the waves would not overwhelm him. So it is with us. Being frightened is part of being alive. The promise

that we could be calm despite the tempest is a promise
on the other side of the seesaw, so to speak. Fear may
push us up into the air, but the knowledge that God
loves us and will support us, and that Jesus will reach
out his hand to us, and tell us, as he did to Peter, "Be
not afraid," will restore the balance.

(Matthew 14:22-33)

We won't be quitters

ACTORS, singers, and TV anchorpersons all seem to have one thing in common these days. If we are to believe the articles about them in the entertainment sections of the papers and magazines, they all require a "break" to succeed. They were working somewhere obscure when someone discovered, or needed a substitute, or decided to take a chance, or just called them because they couldn't find someone else. It wasn't enough that they had talent (and that they are now successful is taken as evidence that they had talent), they also had to have the dogged persistence and tenacity to keep working until they got their "break."

The mythology of "the break" sustains many young people who are still working in obscurity and have persuaded themselves, if no one else, that they have talent. All they need is to be seen by the right person at the right time, and they will be the new Walter Cronkite, Jane Pauley, Sissy Spacek, William Hurt, or Luciano Pavarotti. They are deceiving themselves, of course—at least most of them are. But the possibility of the mysterious, magical "break" is enough to keep them going. The Canaanite woman in the gospel is rather like such people. She, too, was convinced that all she needed for her daughter to be healed would be the right "break." If she could only persuade Jesus, the great healer, to see her and to listen to her, all would be well. She was doggedly and resourcefully persistent and refused to give up until she got what she wanted.

The story has always bothered Christians, for in the

conversation with the Canaanite woman, Jesus really doesn't sound like himself. Since the story does not appear in any of the other gospels, and since it has clearly theological implications for those in Matthew's community who did not want to admit Gentiles, many think that while the incident of the healing of the daughter of the Canaanite woman may well have been based on historical fact, the dialogue is a theological conversation composed by Matthew to make a point. Others think that the story may be a parable of Jesus that was turned by the gospel author into a real event. Still others are persuaded that by the tone of his voice, the gestures of his hand, and the compassion on his face, Jesus indicated his sympathies with the woman and his sensitivity to her request. Jesus was unfailingly kind and gracious to women. Even if he said a seemingly harsh word at the beginning of his dialogue with the Canaanite woman, his attitude and style with her, it is argued, simply could not have been harsh.

Whatever interpretation is to be placed on this unusual story, the fact remains that it often seems that God turns his back on us; and turns his back on our prayers the same way Jesus dealt with the petitions of the Canaanite woman. It is as though God wants to test us to make sure of our faith, to prove our love. In fact God doesn't need to test our faith or prove our love; he knows the quality of both. But oftentimes we need the experience of persistence to strengthen our faith and character. The Canaanite woman, should she really have had the conversation related in the gospel, undoubtedly went home not only rejoicing that her daughter was cured, but also pleased with herself. She had outargued the Jewish healer and then been praised by him for her tenacity and persistence. He said, in effect, that she was one very tough person; and there is no doubt that she would be delighted with the compliment.

So it is with us. God doesn't need our persistence; God doesn't need our dedication; God doesn't need our resourcefulness, our ingenuity, our determination; but oftentimes we do. We need the self-confidence, the self-esteem, the sense of character and commitment that persistence, determination, fortitude display. God is not testing our faith in situations like that in which the Canaanite woman found herself; he is rather giving us an opportunity to develop our religious character. We don't always pretend to understand the whys and the wherefores of such crises; and sometimes we would very much like to be dispensed from such character-building techniques and experiences. Doubtless the Canaanite woman would just as soon not have had to deal with Jesus the way she did. But afterward, when her persistence, her courage, and her resourcefulness paid off, she surely would have said that not only was the outcome worth the effort, but the effort was worthwhile itself. We humans grow through overcoming obstacles, and while that overcoming process may have been unpleasant, the satisfaction of having grown is pleasant indeed.

So whether it is overcoming the harassments of the day, when the telephone doesn't stop ringing, or the crisis of a sick child, or the frustration of a difficult period in a marriage, or the strain of a family budget that simply won't balance, we must doggedly persist both in our efforts to deal with the problems and in our prayers to God for help. We understand that it is precisely in such dogged persistence that we become more fully human, more authentic Christians, and more faithful followers of Jesus. It is the person who keeps trying, no matter how difficult the circumstances and how difficult the solution, that merits the same praise as the Canaanite woman, of whom it was said that in the whole of Israel Jesus did not find such great faith.

(Matthew 15:21-28)

Settling our quarrels

THE message of Jesus is simple and to the point: Settle your fights; don't let your life be burdened by conflicts; minimize the number of enemies and maximize the number of reconciliations. You have better things to do in life than to fight with one another. Alas and unfortunately, there are some of us who seem not to have better things to do in our lives than to engage in quarrels; we seem happiest when we are quarreling. There is a bit in each one of us of Ms. Yokum from the now defunct "L'il Abner" comic strip: "Ah love peace. There's nothin' Ah love more than peace, cept'n maybe a good fight."

We fight with others because we are insecure and threatened, because the behavior of others is a challenge to our freedom, our dignity, our worth, sometimes our very survival. On occasions these threats are real and intended; on other occasions they are imaginary. As the man in Saul Bellow's novel remarked, "Some of us paranoids have enemies." Whether the threat to our being is real or not is much less important than our perception that it is real and the effect it has on us. We are threatened, we must defend ourselves, we fight back. Thus are born both lovers' quarrels and world wars.

Understanding human nature in its imperfect condition, Jesus and the early church took it for granted that there would be conflicts. One might even say that the early church had an intuitive feeling that conflict cleared the air, discharged tension, prepared the way for renewal and reconciliation. Jesus does not say in the gospel: "Don't fight with one another, don't be angry with one another." Rather he says: "Be quick to make peace with one another." The gospel is not for preventing conflict but for facilitating reconciliation.

Reconciliation can only occur, however, when the root causes of a quarrel are understood. Not every lover's spat, obviously, should be analyzed to death. But a persistent pattern of quarrels between those who love one another simply will not be resolved or become the occasion for growth in love if both say "I'm sorry" and try to paper over fundamental differences that have led to the conflict. When lovers quarrel persistently and frequently, both have become a threat, perhaps an awesome threat, to one another. The threat may be, and probably is, due to a misunderstanding, a misperception, a failure in sensitivity and communication; but it is a threat nonetheless. The nature of this threat must be brought out into the open and talked about. That seems to be precisely the strategy the church has in mind in the gospel: "Brothers (for which we might just as well use the word "lovers") must talk to one another about the problem." Men and women can be married for many years, parents and children can live together for many years, not only without developing the skills necessary to articulate the threats that are perceived in their relationship but even more without being aware that such skills are necessary, and that discussing the threats that each perceives in their relationship is both feasible and imperative.

In these days one does not invoke the church the way the community of Matthew did when it had quarrels—at least not directly or explicitly. Nonetheless, when couples are trying to settle their differences, it is still important that they invoke their faith. Dealing with the root causes of quarreling and conflict in an intimate human relationship is one of the most risky and dangerous things a person can do (or at least it seems so before the fact). One needs deep and strong faith in the fundamental goodness of life and in the God who presides over life to be ready to take that risk. The gospel tells us that it is indeed safe to run the risk of forgiving and being forgiven.

The question is not whether there are patterns of conflict in our intimate lives that are covered over by fear, for in every human intimacy there are lots of them. The question in light of the gospel is which particular pattern of conflict, threat, silence, and fear is the one that ought to be addressed first.

(Matthew 18:15-20)

Being truly sorry

YOU have hurt someone else, deliberately or not—forgot to invite them to a party, overlooked their birthday or anniversary, neglected to thank them for a gift, said something facetiously that was taken seriously, didn't appreciate something they had worked hard on. You realize what a terrible thing you have done and quickly but sincerely offer a sorrowful apology. The person listens, nods, and then either rejects your apology outright or simply walks away from you without replying. You have been neither forgiven nor forgotten. You feel embarrassed, humiliated, rejected, and hurt. You begin to store up anger of your own. What right does this person, or any person, have to reject an apology?

In the gospel we learn that those who are so arrogant as not to forgive claim to be superior even to God. However, the strategies for forgiveness vary from case to case—reconciliations have to be based on realistic understandings of what causes conflicts to begin with. The quick and easy forgiveness which ducks the responsibility to sort out what went wrong is not authentic forgiveness. The issue is whether we are willing to forgive, not the process by which we forgive. The servant did not have to remit all of his fellow servant's debt. His refusal to show any mercy at all after he had been treated mercifully was his offense.

All of us need to be forgiven not only by God but by our fellow human beings. There is not one who has not gone blundering through life stepping on toes, hurting feelings, being insensitive, thoughtless, punitive, and just plain obnoxious. Just as he who is without sin can throw the first stone, he who is perfect does not need to ask for forgiveness. Indeed, most of us are very punctilious and demanding when it comes to extracting apologies from others, and very slovenly, tardy, and grudging when it comes to saying, "I'm sorry." Moreover, we expect to be forgiven quickly and completely when we mumble our ungracious apologies, but we also expect detailed, elaborate, obsequious, and totally contrite apologies from those who have offended us. God may be merciful, we seem to think, which is his business, and others had better be merciful to us; but we dish out our own mercy in carefully measured, limited amounts.

Erich Segal, in his book *Love Story*, was just plain wrong when he said "Love means never having to say you're sorry." What love actually means is that one person says, "I'm sorry, forgive me," and the other person says, "I'm sorry too. Forgive me." Love is an endless exchange of apology and forgiveness, sorrow and mercy, forgiveness and being forgiven. Both sides must apologize, both sides must accept apologies; both sides must seek mercy, both must give mercy. The exchange of mercy and forgiveness fosters the growth and flourishing of love.

Who should seek reconciliation first? The ordinary answer is that it is the one who has given the offense. But in most quarrels each side thinks the other has given the offense first; if one waits until the "guilty" party attempts reconciliation, there never will be a reconciliation. The only answer for Christians is that both sides should seek reconciliation first. A strange paradox of human behavior is that the first one to say "I'm sorry" becomes the stronger and the more powerful in the relationship. As one wag remarked, "Oh, I always apologize to my wife before she apologizes to me, because then she's convinced I'm more wonderful than I really am."

In fact, the strategy for reconciliation is not to analyze what the other has done to lead to the quarrel, not to try to find what was the other's blame, but rather to determine one's own blame. In a well-structured relationship, reconciliations are accomplished by the two partners, each of whom acknowledges his or her own guilt instead of accusing the other of guilt. It is hard to establish and hard to sustain this behavior; but it is also the only sure way to guarantee reconciliation. Thus the two servants in the gospel might have had a dialogue something like this:

"Hey, I'm sorry, but, you know, I've been slipshod about paying what I owe you. I just got bogged down in other responsibilities and debts; but I've got things pretty well straightened out now, and I won't be afraid to discuss it with you again."

The response might have been:

"And I haven't been attentive to my responsibility to remind you of the payment, because I was afraid you'd resent it. I'm certainly willing to remit some of your debts if you want me to, or to stretch the payments out. In the future I won't be afraid to remind you."

Mercy, then, means not merely the willingness to forgive, but also the willingness to analyze how each one has contributed to the situation that requires forgiveness. Perhaps there are some circumstances in which our share of the blame is minimal. However, it is very

45

likely that only God can claim immunity from blame in interpersonal conflict. Yet, despite that fact, he is the last one to sit on his high horse and demand that others crawl.

(Matthew 18:21-35)

Can you be too generous?

A GROUP of children have set up a lemonade stand on a hot summer's day. A man walks down the street, buys two glasses of lemonade, gulps them down quickly, and is informed that they are 10¢ apiece. He gives the kids a dollar, says it was delicious lemonade, and walks away. The kids eye him suspiciously. They only asked for 20¢. What's the matter with him? Why has he given them a dollar? A quarter, even a half dollar would be all right. A dollar is too much. They go into the house and discuss the matter with their mother. She frowns. What kind of a man is it who gives a dollar for two glasses of lemonade that isn't all that good anyhow? She warns her children not to sell lemonade to the man if he comes back but to come in and tell her if he tries to give them another dollar. She then calls her next-door neighbor and wonders whether the police ought to be informed. If there's a strange man in the neighborhood who is acting crazy—paying a dollar for two glasses of lemonade—perhaps the police ought to know about it.

Humankind is fundamentally suspicious of generosity. Even limited generosity we think must have strings attached, and the more the generosity appears to be unlimited the more we are convinced that there is some secret design, a nefarious plot, some underhanded scheme at work. People are just not naturally generous, we tell ourselves, which means, of course, that normally we don't feel very generous. When someone breaks all the rules and seems extraordinarily generous without

47

any strings attached we are skeptical, suspicious, frequently snide. The excessively generous person is either up to no good, crazy, or possibly both. Thus it is with the "penny-paying" farmer in the gospel. Not only were those that worked all day offended by his generosity to the loafers who had come along at the last hour, we suspect that the loafers, hostile persons that they were, were also suspicious. They wanted to complain about getting paid enough, and the farmer had undercut their complaints. They must have been very suspicious indeed. What kind of a farmer was it who was so generous that he left them nothing to complain about?

It is generally known today that the story Jesus told was one that was very familiar to his audience, but, as in so many of his stories, Jesus put his own trick ending to it. In the parable that was commonly told by the rabbis, those who came at the last hour worked so hard that they earned as much as those who had worked all day. The emphasis was on their diligence and on the farmer's just recognition of their diligence. In the parable of Jesus, however, the emphasis is not on the diligence of the workers. Quite the contrary, they are presented as rather mean-spirited, scruffy characters. The emphasis is on the excessive generosity of the farmer, a man who had to be crazy or up to no good, or he wouldn't do such a bizarre thing. The farmer was crazy in his generosity, so he earned the enmity certainly of those who had worked through the whole day and possibly of those whom he had overwhelmed with the pay they did not deserve.

The point of the parable, of course, is that by human

standards God's generosity is so excessive as to be deemed crazy. It is such that we humans feel properly suspicious of him. Either we deny the generosity of God, which Jesus came to reveal, by turning him into a harsh, cruel hangman in the sky, or we become very suspicious of God. We decide that God has to be up to no good if he is that nutty in his generosity. Any God that is as generous as the farmer in the gospel story is not a God to be trusted in our cynical view.

In many ways this parable is the most disturbing in the whole New Testament. It doesn't seem fair. When we understand that the emphasis is on God's excessive generosity, it becomes even more disturbing because we don't quite know what to make of a God who has fallen so crazily in love with his creatures. We are not at all sure we want to be the subject of such mind-unhinging love. In a way the theme of the parable is that whether we want to or not, God loves us in the same mad, excessive, exaggerated, generous way that the farmer loved the poor, dumb loafers who needed a day's wages to feed their wives and children. Like it or not, God's excessive generosity is an overwhelmingly important reality in our lives, and we had better learn to adjust to it.

One might well conclude that we have an obligation to be generous to others as God is generous to us. Even if we cannot be as excessively generous as God is, perhaps we might be a little less cynical and skeptical about generous persons; for they might well be motivated by the same emotions that drive God—a deep and powerful love. It may be that the man who gave the little children the dollar for the lemonade had no other motive in mind save delight in little children.

(Matthew 20:1-16)

Not honoring a promise

IN *Limits: The Search for Values* the author argues that after the self-indulgent years of the 1960s and 1970s, when people "did their own thing" and sought "self-fulfillment" and felt free to break commitments in order to promote "personal growth," we have come to a new era in which we recognize the necessary limits in human freedom. We are beginning to take more seriously the need for commitments that are seriously made and honorably kept no matter what the difficulties may be. We are coming to realize that commitments and fidelities are essential to human happiness, and that those who are slaves to the impulses of the moment are every bit as much in prison as those who are caught in the tentacles of legalistic regulations.

We learn about fidelity in the gospel—about keeping commitments, honoring one's word, doing those things that one ought to do not because extrinsic laws, regulations and obligations demand it, but because of the fundamental nature of reality. One honors one's parents; one does those things that parents have a right to expect and which they reasonably ask. The gospel tells us that the important thing is not verbal fidelity, not saying, "Yes, I am committed and I will honor my commitment." The important thing is behavioral fidelity—doing those things which one ought to do not because some law says to but because the nature of one's commitment requires it. The gospel has the same human insight that psychologists have discovered after the last 20 years of narcissism: Human beings can't be happy without making commitments and sticking to them. There are times, of course, when a mistaken commitment can be revised or reconsidered. No one, not even the church today, will insist on the absolute and total irrevocability of commitment. Yet what the psychologists have discovered is that it is essential to human happiness that the presumption should always be in favor of the durability of a commitment once it is seriously made until the case against it is overwhelmingly clear.

In its original Latin sense, fidelity is a strong, positive word that represents loyalty to a commitment. It describes not the things that are not done but the things that are done. However, in English the word has acquired a negative meaning. The faithful husband and the faithful wife do not commit adultery; the faithful lover is one who does not betray love; the faithful public servant is one who does not engage in trickery or corruption; the faithful friend is the one who does not let you down. In fact, however, the faithful friend is the one who actively and positively helps you; the faithful lover is one who deepens, enriches, and strengthens love; the faithful politician is one who vigorously and actively pursues the responsibilities of office; and the faithful spouse is not so much the one who stays out of someone else's bed as one who works to find fulfillment at home. Honoring the commitment of marriage does not mean principally or primarily that you do not get divorced. It means, much more basically and fundamentally, that you do everything possible to promote and facilitate the growth in intensity and richness of your married love.

The problem of the 1960s and 1970s was that people

deceived themselves into thinking that commitment involved merely negative obligations. If that's all it was, then it was distasteful and unattractive, narrow, rigid, and inhibiting. But commitments are not prohibitions; they are rather deep and challenging possibilities. When Jesus made a commitment to someone he promised to do everything in his power to promote growth in affection and dedication and loyalty to the other. Commitment thus perceived is not a restriction or a constraint, but one of the most extraordinary challenges we can face in life. Commitments are not for timid children who are afraid not to do anything else; commitments are for adults who have the strength and the wisdom to accept open and challenging relationships with others.

Commitments, then, do not reduce us to cautious rule-keeping, but challenge us to the depths of our courage, our patience, our skills, our capacity to love. Commitment demands that we do everything in our power to break through the resistance to love within our own personality and that of the one we love. A commitment does not weaken our character development but brings out the best within us. It demands that we be courageous, reckless, romantic. The cowardly, the dull, the prosaic are simply not up to the challenge of commitment. If you do not have the ability to try something new, to start over, to write off the mistakes of the past and begin with a clean slate, you are not ready to accept the enormous challenge of commitment.

(Matthew 21:28-32)

SUICIDES go up during the Christmas holidays; so do homicides, family conflicts, heart attacks, natural deaths. The season of the year which is supposed to be joyous, in which festivity and celebration are supposed to exorcise demons of the long night and the short days in fact seems to produce its own special holocaust of discouraged, tormented, troubled souls for whom the pains of life become especially intolerable. And the great communal festivity lays bare the loneliness, the isolation, the alienation that are characteristic of so many lives. Christmas, it seems, is a time when we want to be loved, we need to be loved, we have to be loved; but it is too often a season not of love but of loneliness, not of unity but of separation, not of joy but of pain and sorrow.

The original Christmas was certainly a lonely time for the participants. Mary and Joseph were away from their home and family, isolated from their friends and community, and forced to live in a cave on a hillside. Jesus came into the world in about as isolated and alienated an environment as possible, for a baby. We romanticize the crib scene now with angels and shepherds and wise men, and livestock too, bathed in heavenly radiance to cover over a harsh, cold, uncomfortable, brutal environment. It is saved from complete inhumanity only by the strong triadic family wall that bound Jesus and Mary and Joseph together. But, of course, this is the most important thing. Jesus, Mary, and Joseph did have one another, and it was, after all, enough. They belonged to something, they belonged to one another; no more is required. And while their love did not make the harshness and the brutality of the hillside scene any easier, it transformed totally the meaning of the environment. People become sick and die or kill themselves at Christmastime because they are convinced that no one loves them, that no one cares, and that, indeed, they are not lovable. This Christmas loneliness affects all of us to some extent. There are twinges of poignant emptiness every once in a while in the course of Christmas time. Our emotions are especially volatile; strains and tensions build up inside our personality, and sometimes it seems that we are all wounds waiting to erupt. Our emotions are stretched like a rubber band about to break. It is as though we all feel that while it is a feast of intimate love, there is a possibility that we are going to be excluded from that love, or at least not fully welcomed into it. Like Willy Loman, in the famous play, *Death of a Salesman,* we may be loved but not well loved. Christmas may be a feast of unity between God and man, between husband and wife, parents and children, but it is also, paradoxically and poignantly, a time of loneliness. Precisely because we want to be loved so much we feel keenly that fundamental distinctiveness and separateness which is part of the human condition particularly at this time. Tears of isolation always lurk just behind the laughter at Christmastime.

We know all the cliches about giving instead of receiving, about the Christmas spirit, of going out to others instead of waiting for them to come to us. At Christmas, oddly of all times of the year, we grow weary of serving instead of being served, we grow tired of giving and want to receive, we have had enough of being responsive and want others to respond to us. We are told that Bethlehem was a fairly harsh place. Somehow that doesn't quite console us, because where we live seems harsh too.

Perhaps we need to rethink our approach to Christmas. Perhaps Christmas ought to be a time of reaching out, of honest, open, and vulnerable reaching out to those whom we love, telling them how lonely and separated and cut off we feel, especially at those times when the noise of the party is the loudest. Instead of pretending that we are carefree and rejoicing, maybe we ought to share with one another our interludes of emptiness and pain during the Christmas season. Does that sound strange? Surely Mary and Joseph must have done that in the cave at Bethlehem. We cannot imagine them complaining about their fate, but neither can we imagine their maintaining an artificial gaity in the face of what must have been a painful and difficult experience. They loved one another. Surely they felt free to express to each other their loneliness, their sense of being outcasts. By so doing they deepened and enriched their lives together, for love grows by sharing the bad times, by revealing our anxieties and fears to those we love; love flourishes when lovers admit their vulnerability to one another.

Obviously Christmas is still a joyous season, a time of festivity and celebration, a time when we rejoice with those whom we love. But only the naive or the dishonest pretend there is no poignancy or no pain at Christmastime. These should not be hidden, should not be repressed, should not be dismissed as dishonorable or unworthy feelings. They are part of the Christmas experience. The transcendence of pain and isolation is part of the Christmas celebration, for it was precisely to break the pain of separation between humankind and God that Jesus came to the world at Christmastime.

(Luke 2:1-14)

Are permanent commitments obsolete?

MANY of the young people who grew up between 1965 and 1975 persuaded themselves that family was outmoded and unimportant. Why was the empty ritual of a public marriage ceremony required to "sanctify" love between a man and a woman? Wasn't the relationship sanctified enough by the fact that they loved one another? And why was it necessary to tie oneself into long-term commitments through marriage and family? Commitments were oppressive to the freedom of women and injurious even to the dignity of men. Why couldn't marriage become a day-by-day commitment which could be dissolved immediately if the happiness of either of the parties required it? There should be no ties that bind, no strings attached, no commitments that could not be repealed. This was the new freedom, the new morality, the sexual revolution, the new feminism—a dramatic change from the old-fashioned irrelevancies of the past.

A very large number of young people (who are not so young any more) are now married, raising children, and forming strong, permanent commitments. Indeed, some of them have become even more familial and more domestic than their parents were. Some of the rhetoric about the sexual revolution and the new morality may remain, but in practice these aging radicals of the late sixties and early seventies have discovered that while the commitments of family life are frequently irksome, difficult and hard to live within, it is even harder to live without them. The only thing worse than a life in which two people are tied together by commitment is one in which there are no ties and no commitments. The only thing more oppressive than the family is not having family.

Biology ties humans together—husband, wife, parent, child. But because we are reflective beings, our biological ties must be reflected and reinforced by personal commitment. And yet commitment is not just a matter of option, not just something we add on like white-walled tires, or FM stereo in an automobile. There are women and men who live together for many years without a marriage ceremony and then discover that separation is every bit as terrible as divorce. A man and woman who relate to each other intimately for a long period of time may think they do so without establishing commitments to one another, but in fact the commitment emerges and is embodied in the involvement of the one person in the other. Similarly, children who argue they no longer have any commitments to their parents because they did not choose them and now they are absolutely independent of their biological ancestors are deluding themselves. The fact that man and woman, parent and child live together in shared experience and intimacy and retain an enormous capacity to hurt one another is sufficient proof, if any were needed, that relationships of intimacy create a powerful propensity, an almost irresistible predisposition, to interpersonal commitment.

What, then, of the "crisis of the family" about which we hear so much? The real crisis of the family is not that it is less important than it used to be but more important. Men and women, parents and children, expect more out of a family relationship than they ever did in the past. The real problem of contemporary family life is that we don't have the skills of generosity, of self-giving, of commitment that are necessary to achieve the expectations we put into our family. Today, we expect the kind of payoffs and rewards from families that are only possible with very deep, very intense and profound commitments to care for each other, to lovingly, tenderly, and sensitively respond to each other, to be sympathetic, patient, gentle with one another. The flower children of the '60s and '70s finally came to understand that commitments are essential to human living. Now, perhaps, some of them are beginning to understand that one can obtain deep, rich and rewarding joy from a relationship only when the commitment is intense, self-sacrificing, kind, open, generous, and more concerned about the happiness of the other than about one's own personal happiness.

The skilled lover is one who has spent a lifetime discovering the needs, the weaknesses, the strengths, the liabilities and the assets, the hopes and the sorrows, the joys and the fears of the other members of his or her family. Such a person can commit himself or herself, then, to the family with resolute and unshakable love. The crisis of the family is that not very many of us are all that good at such love.

There were stresses and strains, joys and sorrows, misunderstandings and reconciliations in the Holy Family—there had to be or they were not a human family. Oftentimes we describe the Holy Family in such terms that it becomes so idealized as to be detached from the human condition altogether. But it is sound theology to believe that the Holy Family grew in love just as all human families, and that Jesus, Mary, and Joseph had to acquire the skills at loving that all families must acquire. We look to them not because they were immune from the struggle which is part of the human condition but because they are an example of love that persists in developing and improving skills and sensitivity no matter what the obstacles and no matter how many difficulties are involved.

(Luke 2:22-40)

The gift of healing

LEPROSY in Jesus' time included not only what we call Hanson's disease today, but all serious infections that manifested themselves in human skin. Measles and scarlet fever, for example, were often fatal diseases in the past. Those and many other ailments were subsumed under the heading of leprosy. Sufferers were quickly banished from the towns. This was, of course, a very cruel if necessary public health measure. It was made all the worse by the fact that people had to justify the cruelty by persuading themselves, and usually the victim of the disease, that it was God's punishment for something they had done wrong.

Local priests in Mosaic law played the role of public health officials. Of course, some of the sick people recovered, some of the diseases went away and there was no need to exclude the healed person from the community. But there had to be some sort of examination to make sure that the person who claimed to be cured and the family who claimed to have a cured person among them were not faking. The ritual of presenting oneself to the priest to be approved had religious overtones, but it was, nonetheless, in its origins in Mosaic law another crude technique of public health. Note well that when someone who had been banished to the garbage dumps on the fringes of town was permitted to return, the community would attribute the cure to God's having forgiven the sin which had created the disease in the first place. The restoration of physical health also meant the restoration of spiritual health. By curing the leper Jesus claimed de facto also to have forgiven the leper's sins.

You can imagine the psychological state of such people. Wives, mothers, children were snatched from their families and forced to fend for themselves among the rocks in the ravine and amidst all the human and non-human terrors that lurked there. Husbands and fathers would be torn from their families, young lovers separated, respected citizens would suddenly become pariahs, people who may have been models of probity were now outcasts and would have to shout "unclean! unclean!" to all passers-by lest their physical and moral contamination spread to the innocent. We may well rejoice that medical science has eliminated such disease for the most part and that we are able to distinguish between physical sickness and moral guilt.

When we read in the gospel about God curing the leper we must realize that the point of the miracle for us today is that we are forgiven. God's forgiveness is there, waiting for us, at all times in our life. It doesn't matter how bad we are, how many mistakes we have made, how horrendously we have fouled up our lives, or the mess we have made of our relationships. The forgiveness is there. It is not that we have to persuade God to forgive us; it is more that we have to accept it. The healing which Jesus offers is a pure gift, not earned, not merited, not won by petition and sacrifice, but rather given freely, generously, spontaneously out of God's love. So, too, is the forgiveness of sins. It is as quick, as easy, as devastating, as decisive as Jesus' words in the gospel: "I will do it. Be cured."

Why, then, do Catholics so often believe God's forgiveness is hard to obtain? Probably the reason is that if forgiveness is hard to come by, we have fewer excuses to avoid transforming our lives, remaking and remodeling our relationships. If God's forgiveness is easily and quickly obtained, then God's demands on us to act as forgiven and renewed human beings is awesome. If Jesus had required the leper who was cured to make enormous sacrifices as preconditions of being restored to his wife and children, then the man could have come back into town proudly as someone who had by himself, more or less, conquered sickness and sin. He could have demanded that his family and friends respect his efforts for the rest of his life. As it was, he was quickly, spontaneously, and easily cured. He would go back into the town as someone who was astonishingly given a precious gift, wondrously blessed with marvelous grace, and hence obliged to be giving and gracious to others for the rest of his life. He had not earned healing; rather he had been overwhelmed by love, and it was incumbent upon him when he returned to the town to overwhelm others with love. We can imagine that it was not infrequent later in his life, as he tried to live up to the great gift that had been given him, that he thought he might be better off if Jesus had not made it so easy and still so difficult.

(Mark 1:40-45)

Growing up

MATURITY, wisdom, poise, experience can't be taught. They have to be learned, and they are almost always learned through mistakes, failure, defeat, humiliation, pain, heartache. It seems to be built into our human nature that we learn much better from our mistakes than from our accomplishments and much more from our failures than from our successes. Even married people, for example, learn the skills that are necessary to love one another only through repeated failure, pain, and frustration. And no love, however powerful or however passionate, is able to substitute for the experience of living together and learning about each other and growing gradually and painfully and slowly in love.

This is the fundamental human insight on which the religious truth in the gospel is based and from which the religious truth is inseparable. We cannot live save by dying, we cannot gain our lives save by being willing to lose them, we cannot succeed save by failing, we cannot grow save by blundering. The person who avoids all risk, all chances, all mistakes, all pain, all frustration will never move off ground zero. Persons who are so uncertain, so insecure that they hunker down to protect their lives, refusing to risk their personhood, refusing to be vulnerable, refusing to take chances will never find a better, deeper, richer life, and will end up losing what little life they already have.

We all must die. Of that there is no mistake. Much of what we do in life is an attempt to avoid dying, to protect ourselves from dying, to establish security around us to keep death at bay, to pretend that there is no death. The more we concentrate on avoiding death, the more rigid and unsatisfying and pointless and unappealing our life becomes. Paradoxically, the more we forget about death and put aside the defenses and the security mechanisms we build up against death, the more vital, the more appealing, the more attractive, the more dynamic we become to others. Being willing to lose our life enables us, in fact, to find it.

There is profound psychological truth in the saying of Jesus that "anyone who loves this life loses it, anyone who hates his life in this world will keep it for eternal life." But the question remains even after we have acknowledged the wisdom of losing life in order to find it. Is it a commonplace or routine experience in daily life to gain life by losing it? Or is it a revelation, a hint of an explanation, a sacrament, a basic and more fundamental existential and theological truth? We all know that we grow through pain, sacrifice, and mistakes, that we begin to live to the new self by dying to the old self, that the more vulnerable, more open, and more defenseless we become the more attractive we are and the more we are rewarded. But is that merely a phenomenon of human living, or is that a Truth structured into the very nature of the universe? It is certainly the case, as Jesus said, that when the seed dies in the ground, something better begins to live. But is that wisdom truly universal? Does it go to the core of what life and existence, the world and the universe mean? Is death the secret of life? Must we always die in order that we might begin to live, even up to and including that final death, the fear of which generates all our other fears of dying? Often we think this might be so, we hope it is so, we half believe it is so. In our best moments, we *know* it is so. Jesus came into the world not to provide us with this insight that death is the prelude to life but to confirm it, to validate, tell us that it is true even beyond our imaginings.

We are all afraid of death, and we will never be able to give up that fear. The question we must ask ourselves today as we reflect on the gospel is not whether we are ready to give ourselves over to life while unafraid of death, but rather are we willing to continue, however hesitantly and imperfectly, to live even though we know we must die. The person who has eliminated all risk from life is the person who has already died. And so we ask ourselves how much the fear of death dominates, controls, and overwhelms our love of life.

(John 12:20-33)

The implications of friendship

THERE'S an old Irish saying that you only know who your friends are when the lights go out in the barroom. It says in a concrete way the wisdom about fair-weather friends. Those who stand by us when we don't need help may or may not be friends; but those who stick with us when we desperately need help are friends indeed. Back in the early 1950s, when Alger Hiss was being accused of being a communist agent, Dean Acheson, who was to become Harry Truman's secretary of state, bluntly told harrassing reporters, "I will not turn my back on Alger Hiss." Acheson was attacked mercilessly by the McCarthyite right wing of the American population and accused of being "soft on communism," if not a communist himself. Oddly enough, in the next two decades, Acheson would also become the target of many liberals who charged he was too anticommunist, a prototypical cold warrior. Indeed, during the Cuban missile crisis, Acheson was one of the hawks who wanted to bomb the Russian missile sites. Acheson was a hawk, but he still did not turn his back on Alger Hiss, for, as he told the reporters in a quotation that was frequently not cited, "I was in prison and you visited me." In other words, a friend is a friend, and you stand by them even when they are accused of treason.

Is there any difference between friendship and love? Sometimes we seem to think that friendship is a step on the way to love, or perhaps a bloodless, passionless variety of love. In fact, however, friendship—defined as unselfish and permanent concern for the good of another

—is the highest form of love. Passion between a man and woman is a prelude, a path, to friendship. Not all friendships are based on sexual love, but any sexual love that does not lead to friendship is bound to be short-lived. Often, too, we use the word "friend" to refer to someone who is merely an acquaintance, that is to say, someone with whom we associate on relatively good terms and with whom we share certain enjoyments. There is nothing wrong with being an acquaintance, but it is a mistake to confuse a friend and an acquaintance. An acquaintance has made no durable commitment to us (and need not make one); an acquaintance is rather someone who has made a temporary, but open-ended, commitment with regard to certain aspects of life. A friend has made a permanent commitment to us as a person in all aspects of our life. Acquaintances may let us down, and we may let them down when the demands of the relationship become too strenuous. Friendship flourishes when its demands are strenuous.

Thus, there are not too many friendships in life. We do not have the time, energy, or the resources to sustain a large number of friendships. Some people may only be friends with their spouse; others may go through life without any friends—perhaps through no fault of their own. Still others may have a fair number of friends, though we might be skeptical of people who claim to have multitudes of friends. Friendship is not a matter of number but of quality. A few solid and consistent friends are much better than a large number of acquaintances we mistakenly define as friends.

Perhaps the best definition of a friend is that the person celebrates our success rather than being envious of it and sorrows with us when we fail rather than being pleased at our being put down. Friendship and envy are absolutely and totally inconsistent. An envious friend is a contradiction in terms. If we feel envy at the success of our friend, then it is a sign for us that we are not, in fact, a friend, and that there is deception and self-deception in the relationship that we have called friendship.

When Jesus told his followers, and through his followers, us, that they were no longer servants but friends, he made an absolute and uncompromising promise to stand by us in the barroom when the lights go out. He will support us with all the power, affection, and love at his command in good times and bad, success and failure, in trouble and in joy. He said, in effect: "Whenever you need me, I'll be there, fighting with you, helping you, sustaining you. No matter how many times you may turn away from me, no matter how unfaithful you may be to our friendship, I will never turn my back on you." The Lord God and his son Jesus will stand by us no matter what we do wrong. They will never be ashamed of us, never repudiate us, never run out on us; because they are our friends.

Friendship, in other words, is an interpersonal blank check, a promise of commitment with no strings attached and no holds barred. Friends are sometimes not easy to bear, because they won't go away, they won't let us revel in self-pity or self-hatred. They won't let us quit, they won't let us paralyze ourselves with remorse and guilt. Our friends will not desert us when we fail or do wrong, but they nonetheless demand the best of us, and they are never satisfied with less than best. Friends are a joyous burden; they chain us and bind us because they do not permit us to run away either from them or from that which is best in ourselves. Such is the nature of the friendship that Jesus commits himself to in the gospel today. He accepts the worst in us and demands the best; he stands by us when we are in trouble and challenges us when we are complacent. He will never let us go either at those times when we desperately need a friend nor at those times when we would dearly like to be free of the help of friends.

(John 15:9-17)

Why do we envy success?

WHO is the most successful person that you went to school with? Think about it for a moment. Is it a man who made a lot of money? A woman who made a brilliant marriage? The mother or father whose children are bright, attractive, and affectionate? Someone who has kept their good looks despite the passage of time? Somebody who has become famous? Someone who has a beautiful home, a couple of very expensive cars, or does a lot of traveling? Someone who is popular and successful? How do you feel toward that person? How do you react when you encounter him or her in a chance meeting, or at an occasion like a class reunion? Are you furious that the other person seems to have had a better life than you? Do you eagerly look for the flaws, the imperfections, the sufferings and frustrations in that person's life?

Envy is one of the three or four most powerful human emotions. Hunger, self-preservation, perhaps curiosity, are the only motivations more powerful. Envy is the great ugly secret about which we rarely speak, which all of us feel but few of us acknowledge. The envious person is offended at the success of others and does all in his/her power to deprive them of their success and punish them for it. It is perhaps the most destructive of all human emotions. It strives to destroy the person who is envied, but its nasty, vicious hatefulness also destroys the person who envies.

Envy is universal. We can hate public figures—athletes, movie stars, presidents and their families, the

rich, the famous, the wealthy—because they are successful and we are not. Or we can envy our neighbors,
our relatives, our friends because they seem to have
more power, wealth, popularity, or acclaim than we do.
And always envy takes on a tone of nasty self-righteous-
ness. The people whom we envy do not deserve their
success, we tell ourselves (and others) because they are
morally inferior. (By implication, they are morally inferior to us.) What was so special about Jesus, the citizens of Nazareth asked righteously. He was no better
than anyone else, and yet here he was preaching and
working wonders and attracting crowds. This was
wrong, evil, and unfair—Jesus was no one special. The
citizens of Nazareth had the moral obligation to tell as
many people as they could that Jesus was no one special. The envious person always has the pose of self-
righteousness. He or she pretends to be a plain, simple,
honest person defending integrity, responsibility, maturity, morality, and common sense. Beneath this pose
is a nasty, vicious, destructive hatred.

The most destructive of envies, however, are not
those that are aimed at the greats of this world, though
we do our best to make them suffer, but the ones that
are aimed at those closest to us. It is not at all uncom-
mon for a mother to envy her daughter's beauty or social
success, or a father to envy his son's athletic ability,
career promise, or popularity. Husbands frequently resent even the relatively minor acclaim their wives receive for doing something well; and wives, not infre-
quently, are angry and frustrated at the recognition
their husbands receive. There are all kinds of subtle
ways of punishing the intimate other, the most power-

ful of which may well be silence. We ignore the other's enthusiasm or downplay it or dismiss it with faint praise. We silently pick up the newspaper and begin to read in response to the other's enthusiasm. Such reactions are ridiculous, of course, for the other's success or popularity or achievement or attractiveness has not been purchased at a cost to us. In fact, it reflects favorably upon us. But the envious person does not think logically for all his/her pretense of rationality. If the other has something that we don't have, envy whispers in our ear. That which the other has somehow has been taken from us. We become as mean and as nasty as we can hoping to teach parent, spouse or child never again to offend us by being more successful than we have been, and warning that whatever success is attained will have to be purchased at a very heavy price.

Envy seeks to undermine, to cut down, to constrain and to restrain, to damage, to hurt, to inflict pain and suffering, to reduce everyone and everything to a common level of mediocrity. The world would be an infinitely better, wiser, and more abundant place than it is if it had not been for the enormous restraints that envy has placed even on the most simple and unimportant manifestations of excellence. Envy threw Jesus out of Nazareth; envy crucified him. Each of us in our bursts of envy show the offense we have taken over someone else's goodness, excellence, or accomplishments and try to crucify the person who is the object of our envy.

(Mark 6:1-6)

Sometimes it takes courage

REMEMBER the first time you were on an airplane trip, or the first time you jumped into the water and tried to swim, or the first time you asked a girl for a date, or the first time a boy invited you on a date, or the day you left home to go away to school or into the service, the first day at work, the first test in high school or college. Remember all those times in life when you would have much preferred to say no, play it safe, refuse to risk anything. Yet, for one reason or another, sometimes very reluctantly, you didn't say no; you said yes, took the risk, did what had to be done no matter how scary and even though it might not work out (and sometimes it didn't). The name of the game when you say "yes" even when the prospects are scary is courage.

For someone who has played such an important role in human history, Mary, the mother of Jesus, is not very well known. We have no idea what she looked like, when she was born, when or how she died, or how she spent most of her life. The stories we have in scripture reveal very little and are usually heavily overlaid with theological or religious points the evangelist wanted to make about Mary's son. Perhaps the most effective way of knowing Mary is to study Jesus. As the author puts it in his book *The Mary Myth*, from the kind of man Jesus was we can surmise much about the kind of woman Mary, his mother, was. However, we do know that the strong conviction of 2,000 years of Christian history is that Mary was a woman who said "yes" to God and on that depended everything else that was to happen in the drama. It is not likely that Mary herself spoke the words of the Magnificat. She probably could not have guessed that future generations would call her blessed. Nor is it likely that whoever composed the hymn and put it on her lips comprehended how prophetic the words would be. Yet there is no more accurate prediction in scripture. Precisely because she was a woman of great courage who could say yes to God no matter what the risks, all generations have called her blessed.

Many of us learned in our school days that Mary knew from the beginning that her son would die on the cross, and that when she said yes to the angel she accepted even that tragic ending. While we cannot rule out completely that possibility, it does seem, however, that Mary only had the vaguest notion of what would happen to her and to her son, at least as far as the details were concerned. She did know, she must have known from the very beginning that faith, hope and courage were to be required of her, that there would be terrible suffering, loneliness and pain. One must assume that Mary cared rather little for the honor she may also have sensed would be involved in her yes. We must be content with the basic insight which Christianity in all its denominations has never doubted: Mary knew, perhaps not in specific detail, and with absolute certainty that God was inviting her to assume a very tough, very difficult and demanding task. Unhesitatingly she said, "Yes." Indeed, not only did she say it unhesitatingly but eagerly, confidently. Mary may have been only a teenager—15, 16, 17 years old at the most; she may not have been able to read and write, and she surely had very primitive ideas of geography, science and other disciplines we consider to be important. Nonetheless she had character—more character than any woman who has ever lived.

Most of us say yes to God's invitations at least some of the time. Other times, when we have a choice to make, and say yes rather than no, we do so sluggishly, hesitantly and complainingly. The difference between us and Mary, the mother of Jesus, is that she didn't feel sorry for herself, she didn't complain, she didn't hesitate. Her yes wasn't grudging or complaining. She simply said yes quickly, calmly, effectively, because she knew God loved her and trusted in that love whatever demands her response would impose upon her. It is important that we understand that Mary could have said no, or a grudging all right. We must not make her into a marionette, a puppet, a doll-like creature who had been programmed as a robot in order to respond properly and play her assigned role in the drama God had worked out.

Mary knew the meaning of fear, of uncertainty, of discouragement, of loneliness. It was nowhere written in the stars that her response to God's invitation had to have such character. Her calm acceptance of whatever God wanted, regardless of the challenge and the suffering, the heartache and the pain involved, was in some fundamental sense a response to the same question that each one of us is asked at times in our lives. The courage she showed is not qualitatively different from the courage that is required of us. Neither the challenge, the danger, nor the desire to respond is qualitatively different between us and the Blessed Mother. God asks all of us to make a leap in the dark of fear, loneliness, pain, anxiety, and trust his goodness and love. And he expects us to do it with all the character, all the class and style, all the confidence and elegance, all the promptness and enthusiasm at our command. Mary's "behold, the handmaid of the Lord," is all the more impressive than the response "yes" from the rest of us. But the challenges are not fundamentally different; if they were, Mary would be no help to us as a model of the "character" that is possible in the Christian life.

(Luke 1:39-56)

The real "bad" language

IF you were asked which was the worst abuse of the gift of speech—obscene language, scatalogical language, both of which are most often expressed in four-letter words; the use of God's name in vain; or uncharitable conversation about others—what would you decide? It is much to be feared that many of us would pick the four-letter words first; then the use of "damn," "hell," and (more serious) an occasional "god-damn;" and finally, as the most trivial, uncharitable conversation about other human beings. However, in fact, scatalogical and obscene words, to say nothing of "hell" and "damn," however inappropriate they may be in certain contexts and however much they may be a matter of taste and no taste, are not sins at all. While taking God's name in vain is sinful, God can defend himself from our misuse of the gift of speech. Other human beings, though, can be hurt by sins of uncharitable speech, which is a failure of love; and this is the worst sin of all. Yet we gossip, spread rumors, question motives, impugn integrity, and malign the reputation and character of others—our working colleagues, our friends, our neighbors, and even our parents, children and spouses. Need it be said that there is a certain kind of Christian, not limited to any generation, as we might like to think, who is profoundly offended by the use of four-letter words and yet thinks nothing of routinely demolishing the reputation and character of a friend, neighbor or colleague—all done to a most moral and self-righteous tone.

Andrew M. Greeley

The point of this observation is not to defend vulgarity or tastelessness, but to indicate that it is a curious kind of mentality which strains at the gnat of vulgarity and swallows the camel of uncharitableness. You may well object to the use of four-letter words, particularly by young people and in literature; you are perfectly right to do so. Indeed, you may contend with some reason that the spread of coarse and vulgar language is an indicator of, and perhaps even the cause of, a decline of civility in human discourse and manner. Civility, manners, courtesy are important human attributes. Only don't confuse them with Christianity, which is a religion concerned with a love of God and a love of our fellow human beings. God's name ought to be respected and the character, reputation and integrity of fellow human beings ought to be respected too. If someone should spit out a string of four-letter words right after mass today, you might quite properly be offended. They had just received the Eucharist on their lips and now they are being coarse and vulgar. They really don't do much harm, however, save to their own image and to others' peace of mind. They certainly do nothing to violate the sanctity of the Eucharist. If, however, you should encounter someone who immediately wants to tell you the latest scandal, the latest rumor and gossip about people you both know and don't like, many would not be offended at all. But such conversation sins against charity and violates Christian unity of which the Eucharist is a sacrament.

Children learn their language from their parents. While occasionally they may use street language to offend their parents, it is rare that over the long haul they will use language that parents do not use either publicly or privately when they think the kids aren't listening. If you don't like coarse, vulgar or street language in your house, then don't use it yourself! Many parents are very sensitive to this issue and take offense when somebody else, particularly some other parent's child, uses such language in the presence of their children. But rare indeed is the parent who protests uncharitable conversation from a guest, from someone else's child, or even from a spouse. Somehow that doesn't seem wrong. Don't say four-letter words around the kids, but gossip for hours. That's how we develop young Christian gentlemen and gentlewomen.

If the man whose power of speech and hearing was given back by Christ, as told in the gospel of Saint Mark, had used his newly-found speech to blaspheme God, we would be shocked—and rightly so. If he had developed a foul mouth, we would be horrified; for even though a foul mouth is not nearly so bad as blasphemy, it is still inappropriate, particularly for someone to whom speech is a special gift. But would we be shocked at all if he used his recovered powers of speech to badmouth his neighbors, to tear down their characters, their reputations, their integrity? Probably not, because we tend to do that all the time ourselves and are not unduly offended by it in others. Moreover, there is some reason to think, given the way human nature acts, that if Jesus had come upon the man after he had been cured and heard him speak foully, the man would be acutely embarrassed and would have apologized profusely. But if Jesus had come upon the man badmouthing the man next door the man might scarcely be embarrassed at all. And why do we put other people down? Mostly because we are not satisfied with ourselves. By punishing other people and depriving them of their reputation, by dragging their name in the mud we somehow assure ourselves that we are not all that bad. What else is our power of speech for?

(Mark 7:31-37)

Teenagers versus parents

THE principal causes of conflict between middle-class parents and their teenagers are not drink, drugs, sex, or violence. All these issues of the generation gap pale into insignificance when one considers how parents and teenagers struggle over keeping their rooms neat. While there are some paragons of adolescent perfection, however, who do keep their rooms neat without being told, the state of the teenager's room is often a daily subject of conflict between parent and child.

It can be said with considerable confidence that the older the teenager the less parental authority is likely to work, and it is reported that with the waning of parental authority comes an increase of wisdom, rationality, and cooperation during the teenage years. It often seems that in the interlude between young adolescence and maturity nothing at all motivates the young person except, perhaps, the pressures of friends. During this phase, however, the young person might very well decide to clean up the room. The wise parent quickly learns that making an issue of room neatness only provides a cause for displaying independence. Constant nagging about the room has about as much impact as water on a duck's back.

Our meditation, however, is not concerned with strategies for winning neatness from teenagers. Probably the best way to do that over the long haul (although it doesn't work necessarily in the short run) is for the complaining parent to keep the rest of the house so neat that the young person learns by example and not by word. And this can be the key to other problems. The way Christians exercise authority can be much more influential than the laying down of rules and expectations.

In the gospel we find advice for the leadership of the early church derived from the teaching of Jesus but applied concretely and specifically to the condition of the early Christian community. This suggests that problems with abuse of authority began in the church shortly after Jesus went home to the heavenly Father, and that contemporary authority conflicts are only the most recent manifestations of a long tradition of conflict. First we might be inclined to wonder why. Jesus provided an unmistakable model of authority—the person with authority does not give orders, rather he or she serves and wins the cooperation of others by the generosity, the gentleness, and the sensitivity of his or her service. The model derived by Jesus has not been popular. The specific formulations in the gospel were undoubtedly put down as they are precisely because some of the leaders of the church either did not understand the Jesus model, or, understanding it, did not like it or were afraid to try it. The words are as valid for the way we exercise leadership in the church and family today as they were in the time of Jesus. Popes give orders to bishops, who give orders to pastors, who give orders to curates, who give orders to people; husbands try to give orders to wives, wives frequently give orders to their husbands, and parents give orders to children. Oftentimes nothing gets done, and we are dismayed when our orders don't get obeyed.

When Life Hurts

In the final analysis people won't obey orders unless they want to. Sometimes they want to because a gun is pointed at their head, or they will lose their job, or their family will break up, or they will be grounded on weekends. Fear, in other words, can motivate compliance; but, as has been demonstrated recently in Poland, compliance imposed by force is not very effective. The message of Jesus—example, service, and love—is anything but impractical. On the contrary, over the long run it is a much more effective way of governing, particularly in voluntary organizations where you don't have guns, the secular arm, or the Inquisition any more. The statement of the Declaration of Independence that the authority of government depends upon the consent of the governed is true in all human institutions, not necessarily as a philosophical, ethical, or theological statement but as a practical observation. You have got to get people to go along.

The teenagers who complain most about the arbitrary regulations and rules of parents are very likely to be the most arbitrary when they try to regulate their own children. When the subordinate in the occupational world finally becomes the boss, an absolutely safe predictor of what kind of boss he or she will be can be found in attitudes that person held toward the boss when he or she wasn't one. The person always complaining about the superior, in others words, is in turn likely to become a superior who generates a lot of complaints. To put the matter somewhat differently, we delight in examining ad nauseum the way other people abuse authority and resolutely refuse to examine at all our own abuse of authority. And all of us have authority, down to the youngest child in the family who has not yet found a little sibling to order around.

But, some will argue, after all, I am the boss; I am the grown-up, I am the father, I am the pastor, I am the bishop. I have the right and the duty to give orders, and other people have the right and the duty to obey me. Oh, do you? That doesn't seem to be the way that Jesus, who had more authority than anyone ever, seemed to think or act. Jesus won others to him by love, service, generosity, and kindness and not by laying down the law. Obviously there are rules that must be enforced for the protection of home and family, property and society. The little child must not touch the electrical socket, the teenage girl must not wander around strange, unknown neighborhoods by night; bylaws are necessary for the smooth, harmonious functioning of any human institution or there will be chaos. But authority does not mean, in the Christian view of things, the right and privilege to bend others' wills to one's own. It means, rather, the responsibility and the obligation to win others to cooperation through generosity, love, kindness, and service. If this teaching of Jesus was taken seriously, men and women might not be quite so eager for authority.

(Mark 10:35-45)

Are you satisfied with your life?

CONSIDER the migratory birds who fly south for the winter. Unlike some truculant Canadian geese who have so fallen in love with some northern city areas that they no longer commute between Canada and North Carolina but hang around all year, most migratory birds have the great good sense to head south when their built-in thermometers tell them it is getting cold. They are programmed instinctively to escape from the cold weather, and they do not have to reflect on whether their vacation will interfere with their careers, whether it will be hard on the families, or whether they will return happy or depressed. Only human beings are capable of reflecting on their own emotional state and acting against their own spontaneous impulses when convinced they would be happier, for instance, by not commuting to the sunbelt. No other creature self-consciously pursues happiness. We pursue it all the time.

Jesus came to tell us how to be happy, like every other great moral and religious teacher. "Follow my way," or "follow me," says the religious teacher, "and you will achieve happiness." Jesus, however, took a different tack. He did not lay down detailed moral guidelines, obedience to which would guarantee a happy life. Quite the contrary, Jesus argued that happiness came from knowing the Father in heaven, from understanding God's love. While there were behavioral consequences from knowing the Father as he revealed himself to Jesus, they were not rules and regulations for knowing the Father or for achieving the self-discipline to be able to pray to the Father. For Jesus, religious knowledge was not the end of a life of self-discipline; it was rather the beginning of a life of generosity and service. Christians behave the way they do, if they are truly followers of Jesus, not to be able to understand God or to win God's love, but because they already understand God, they have already experienced his love.

Thus, the formulae for blessedness in the Beatitudes from the Sermon on the Mount are not an ethical code to be compared to the Mosaic Law, the Babylonian Law, or the law of the Greek philosophers. Jesus was *not* an ethical teacher like Moses, Hammurabi or Socrates. The Beatitudes are not a set of new and tougher commandments added as a sort of supplementary obligation to the ten existing commandments; rather they are an existential and empirical description of how people will spontaneously behave when they know the Father and experience his love. They are no more a legal code than the patterns of behavior which a man and woman who deeply love one another establish in their lives when they manifest their love for one another. "Protocol" between married lovers is not a code of legalistic rules and regulations, not a set of conditions through which love is earned; it is rather a natural and spontaneous result of the ever-deepening affection between a man and woman whose love for one another impels them to know each other better, and whose knowledge deepens and strengthens their love. Those of us who observe such people will say that their affectionate behavior is the result of love and not a body of legislation which makes love possible. Thus, the Beatitudes are an empirical description of loving behavior. "If you know the Father and respond to his love as I reveal it to you," Jesus says in effect, "then this is what you will do—not as a way of becoming happy but as a result of the happiness you already experience."

Leaving aside the complicated scriptural question of the exact meaning of each of the Beatitudes, we can summarize them all by saying that they come to: "Happy are they who lovingly serve those around them, because they reveal God's love to others." Living the life of faith, in other words, does not so much require that one keep a new set of rules that are even stricter than the ten commandments, but rather that one be so consumed by the joy of God's love that one spontaneously reflects that love through the generous service of others. Saints do not keep every single rule all the time; they overflow with joy and love and happiness, and in the excitement and passion and power of their love affair with God they give themselves enthusiastically and generously to the kind of service that goes beyond all rules and regulations.

The life of the Beatitudes, then, is one that reveals the presence of God's love. It is not a spiritual ideal to be striven for in order that we might be happy or a concrete description of how happy people live. To the extent that our lives are lives of generous and loving service of others, then we know that we are happy; and to the extent that our lives are turned in on ourselves with little or no concern for others, then we know that our lives are unhappy. The life of the Beatitudes is an indicator, a thermometer of the quality of our love. It no more causes God to love us than the mercury in a thermometer causes heat or cold. The saint is not a man or woman who breaks no laws and bends no regulations; the saint is a person consumed by joy, a joy so powerful and so passionate that it must be shared with others. Fortunately for all of us it is not necessary to be numbered among "all the saints" that we display the passionate love of the life of the Beatitudes every moment of our lives. The more we do live a life of the Beatitudes the happier we will be, or, more precisely, the greater will be the happiness that we reveal in our lives.

(Matthew 5:1-12)

Old age is not for sissies

WHAT are the signs of aging? You walk upstairs instead of running; you can't stay out all night without feeling the effects the next day; it's much harder to deal with a weight problem; you have to buy reading glasses or bifocals; some friends or relatives your own age die; your teeth are not quite as sound as they used to be; your friends whom you haven't seen for awhile seem to have aged notably—especially your classmates at reunions; you have children who are teenagers and then suddenly you have grandchildren; you count up the years of your life and realize that the majority of them have already been lived; and, of course, with each passing year, time seems to go by more quickly rather than less.

When Jesus points out, with more than a little irony, that the blossoming fig tree is a sure sign of the changing seasons, the passing of winter and the nearness of summer he was obviously warning his apostles and those who came after that it was later than they thought —perhaps much later than they thought. It is later than we think—day by day we are closer to a final accounting of our lives, closer to having the quality and effectiveness of our love judged by God. If we are intelligent and if we are prudent, we read the signs of the times, understand that we are getting older, and resolve that we will do the best we can with whatever remains to us. We know that we should live lives of intensity, of commitment, of joy, and of love, instead of being content with dull, commonplace mediocrity. Jesus is not trying to scare us; nor does he suggest that God is an accountant who keeps careful books on everything we do. Rather, Jesus is trying to persuade us to be alert, enthusiastic and eager so that we may not waste the wonderful opportunity that we have been given in our lives. The year winds down and the days grow shorter. In many parts of the country the snow begins to fall and our thoughts naturally turn, if we permit them, to the shortness of our life. However, there is a strong temptation not to permit ourselves to think that way and we force ourselves blindly through the holiday season with no time for stock-taking, for evaluation, for reflection, for rereading the signs of the times, and for realizing that it is later than we think.

Jesus was possessed by a sense of the intimate closeness of God and his sense of urgency includes that sense of intimacy. No matter what our age or what our accomplishments, there is still so much to do. In fact, it seems, the faster we go, the further behind we get; the more we get done, the more there is to do. But the urgency of today's gospel message is not equated with nervous frenzy. Jesus is portrayed in the gospels as living a life of singular purpose, constantly aware of his choices, his possibilities, his decisions. It seems, on the other hand, that we often drift in and out of that condition of total awareness. Sometimes we are in full command; at other times we coast. Indeed, it demands a certain discipline or training to maintain a consistently high level of awareness for a prolonged period of time. This is true in our play, our work, our relationships, our prayer. (And sometimes we sacrifice one—or more —for the other.) A good example of this would be a baseball team (or football, basketball, hockey, etc.) that practices a certain situation over and over so that when it happens in a game situation the players instinctively handle it with ease. Jesus is saying, improve your instincts, stay awake, love one another—you do not know the hour.

There is so little time and so much to do, and somehow we let the unimportant interfere with the essential. We do things we feel we "have" to instead of the things we "should" do; we do the things we "ought" to do instead of what the best in us "wants" to do. We resolve each year not to let the headlong rush of the holiday season interfere with a prayerful and spiritual Christmas. Then, of course, we devote our time and energy to all the obligations we have except the obligations to God and to ourselves. We sigh wistfully when the Christmas tree comes down after the first of January and promise ourselves that next year it will be different.

We procrastinate and put things off. We wait until the kids are in school or out of school; we wait until Labor Day, then Thanksgiving; we wait until the snow stops and then wait until summer; we wait and wait. The sands flow through the hourglass, life slips through our fingers, and the signs of the times are ignored. Jesus keeps warning us each year as the church, with a fine sense of timing, has us listen to these "apocalyptic" gospels. It is just that time of the year when the signs of our time, the signs of our ebbing life, are most obvious and most earnestly ignored.

It is later than we think.

(Mark 13:24-32)

93

The old order is always changing

YOU wake up at night, on vacation perhaps, in a strange place; you are lost on a road you have never traveled before; you are settling in a new home, the kids are complaining like crazy, the telephone is ringing, and there has been a power failure; a snowstorm or a flood has paralyzed traffic; a president has died or resigned; you are trying to go through a stack of bills and records to figure out your income tax—all are experiences of disorganization, of chaos. They generally mark the breakdown of established order and the beginning of something new. Whenever something old is dying and something new is being born there is chaos, confusion, disorder. It is like bring a new baby home from the hospital.

The apocalyptic rhetoric which was common in the time of Jesus, and which Jesus himself used sparingly, presented the profound conviction of the people of that era that the old order was dying and a new order being born (a conviction by no means limited to the Jews). Among many Jews and gentiles of the time, the rhetoric of apocalypse was the rhetoric of hope. The old world had failed. It was oppressive, blasphemous, evil, to be swept away, as John the Baptist thought, in a cleansing fire. Then the new era would begin, the new creation. There was already chaos; there would be more chaos, out of which would emerge the new order. Jews fell back on the creation stories of their tradition, some of which are to be found in Genesis. When the Holy Spirit hovered over the primal chaos, the waters teemed with life. There was disorder and confusion but raw vitality. Then the Spirit intervened and God created and the world of order began. There is also apocalyptic rhetoric to be found in the gospel of St. Luke. It should be understood as a parallel to the early chapters of Genesis, a prediction of the ending of an old creation and the beginning of a new one.

A new order was indeed born in those times but not with the dramatic apocalyptic suddenness the language of the time seemed to indicate. Rather it began in Bethlehem, slowly, gradually, subtly. The world learned, or ought to have learned, that new creations were not like primal "big bangs," but rather gradual and organic changes brought about as the development of human knowledge and love. The old world dies and the new world is born every day. Chaos replaces the tattered, collapsing old order and generates a bright new order each morning of our lives and each week, each month, and each year. In the wonderful words from Sean O'Casey's *Juno and the Paycock*, things are always "in a state of chassis." The old is dying, the new is being generated. There is always another chance, always a new beginning, always a fresh start—at least for those who are quick enough, brave enough, and eager enough to seize the opportunities.

The catch is that we humans do not like disorder. We find ourselves living in a world where chaos seems to be lurking just around the corner and where the divine order that God has imposed on things does not seem obvious enough to make our lives secure and safe. Therefore, we work eagerly to impose neat, orderly, and regular patterns on our existence. This behavior is understandable and acceptable so long as our propensity for order does not become obsessive, does not dull the spontaneity of our spirit and does not squeeze out of our lives the capacity to listen to the Holy Spirit when he whispers words of renewal, inspiration, and creativity.

The problem is that we overreact and rigidify our lives to exclude disorder (though it still continues to creep in under the door) and thus also exclude any opportunity for growth, renewal, rebirth. Quite simply, we refuse to run the risk of permitting the old to die and thereby preclude the possibility of the new being born. In the marriage relationship (to take the most obvious example) chaos threatens even when we pretend that it does not. The strains, the tensions, the needs, the aspirations, the hopes and the fears of the marriage partners can swirl around in a bubbling cauldron. Husband and wife pretend that the waters are cool, ruling problems and opportunities off the agenda without discussion. The marriage may be, then, peaceful and calm; but it is also moribund. There is no conflict, no confrontation, no problems of any sort; but there are also no goals, no creativity, no new discoveries, no renewals of interest, no rebirths of romance or love. Afraid of the chaos that lies around and through all intimacy, the partners refuse to take chances, routinize the relationship and impose on it a rigidity that indeed excludes disorder but also life. Unless the husband and wife are prepared to reevaluate the tattered old order that holds their marriage together, there is simply no way a new order of greater and richer love can possibly be reborn.

We can minimize the chaos in our life, but by so doing we also minimize the creativity.

What is true of marriage can be true of everything in our existence. There is a danger that some people, particularly young people, may go through a hippielike period in which their life is pure chaos. There is an opposite danger for most of us, particularly after a certain age, to settle into established patterns and routines which represent the exact opposite—stagnancy. But Christ challenges us to let the old order die that the new might be reborn, to run the risk of transient chaos and let the new within us and within our relationships be born. Bethlehem, in other words, was not a single event that involved just three people; it is a possibility for all of us each day of our lives.

(Luke 21:25-28, 34-36)

Two kinds of sorrow

THERE are two kinds of sorrow: strategic sorrow and authentic sorrow. Strategic sorrow, for example, is that of the teenager who is sorry because otherwise he or she is likely to be grounded for the next month. Or the man who is late coming home from work because he had a "few drinks with the boys." He's sorry too, because the alternative is a very unpleasant and uncomfortable existence at home.

Parents and spouses are wise enough to take strategic repentance with a grain of salt. In fact, most of our apologies, most of our expressions of regret, most of our repentances are of this variety—at least in substantial part. There may be a touch of meaning, a touch of feeling, a touch of sincerity in our apologies and our repentances; but we offer them because they are expected, because they soothe over the hurt and angers of life, and not because we sincerely regret the pain we have caused. Typical teenagers are sorry they got caught and perhaps sorry that they have unsympathetic parents. Tardy husbands are sorry they had the one last drink, because returning home fifteen minutes sooner might have avoided wifely wrath. We are sorry that there is trouble, that there is fuss, or that we have miscalculated; but we are not really sorry that we have hurt the other.

The repentance that John the Baptist calls for in the gospels is a "metanoia," a total, complete, and profound transformation of the personality. It was not enough, according to the Baptist, to express sorrow and to announce that one has amended one's life. Going down into the waters of the Jordan and being washed by the Baptizer meant not merely an act of contrition but a firm and profound commitment to avoid doing those evil things one did in the past. The waters of the Baptist signified that the baptized person intended to transform utterly and completely his personality. If our late-arriving-home teenagers were to descend into the Jordan River, they would be saying symbolically that they would do everything possible not to worry parents by staying out beyond the deadline, even if it meant offending friends, dates, and other important persons in their lives. And the offending husbands, should they descend into the waters of the river, would be saying symbolically, "At most one drink and then I'm on my way home." The repentance the Baptist demanded, in other words, was not a perfunctory expression of sorrow but rather total renewal of life.

In the catechism lessons of an earlier day we learned that the sacrament of penance was valid only when the act of contrition included "firm purpose of amendment." Often the whole process was legalistic and technical. We detailed our sins, we promptly asserted that we would try not to do them again, in return for which the priest gave us absolution and we were free to receive Holy Communion the next day. We did not, however, really intend to transform our lives—not of the sort John the Baptist has in mind. Perhaps the routine of weekly or monthly confessions demanded so many transformations that none of the individual ones seemed all that important, or maybe it was that we knew that most likely we would all too soon slip back into the same faults all over again no matter how hard we tried.

Authentic repentance, true sorrow, stands somewhere between perfunctory verbal commitment and complete perfection in living up to our commitment. Transformation means serious, determined, and powerful effort; it does not mean either total success or total absence of effort. The teenager will slip again, as will the tardy husband; but the worried parent and the offended spouse can tell how serious the efforts are, if by no other way than diminishing frequency of offense. Metanoia, transformation, is a gradual, organic process of growth—but not so gradual that there is no need for periodic, determined and powerful renewals of our commitment.

It is interesting to note the difference between the motivation for transformation in the preaching of the Baptist and the preaching of Jesus. John knew that the times were critically important, that wonderful events were stirring, that a new era was about to be born, that the old would die and the new would come to life. But his vision of the coming change was fiery, devastating, destructive. Those who did not transform themselves would be wiped out in an all-consuming blaze. You responded to the Baptist's demand for metanoia because he scared the living daylights out of you. You transformed yourself, however, in response to the message of Jesus not because you were frightened by a vision of consuming fire but because you were powerfully attracted by a vision of overwhelming, powerful, seductive love.

The vision of Jesus was not only more beautiful, it was also more realistic about human nature; for fear can transform us for just so long, and then its effectiveness declines dramatically. Love, however, grows in its power as a motivational factor with the passage of time. A husband who is only afraid of his wife's anger will not be able to resist the temptation to action which will infuriate her; and a teenager who merely fears his or her parents, or whose attitude is primarily characterized by fear, will fail over the long haul to maintain a sincere intention to change. Only the loving spouse and the loving teenager, who clearly and deeply do not want to hurt the ones they love, will be able to sustain a purpose of amendment. Jesus preached love because the heavenly Father he knew was a God of love. He also preached love because he knew that in the final analysis love was the only motive that worked. The fear of the Lord is the beginning of wisdom but love is the end, the summation of wisdom.

(Luke 3:10-18)

Are we prepared to talk about it?

REMEMBER, if you can, a particularly bitter family row with your husband, your wife, or your children—not necessarily the one that happened this morning, last night, or even last week; but a really monumental blowup. Think about what went into that fight. Often it was triggered by some minor accident that aggravated bitterness and resentment that had been building up for weeks, months, or even years. And sometimes, perhaps rather often, that about which you fought was not that which really made you angry.

Serious family conflicts usually are caused by a combination of two factors: (1) impatience over the fact that other intimate persons are different than you are; and (2) inability to communicate about this impatience. If something that our spouse, our parents, or our children do drives us up the wall, that is inevitable, normal, part of the human condition. But if we cannot or will not talk about this problem, then we are doing the same thing psychologically that we would do in our home physically if we were to soak the basement with gasoline and scatter combustible rags around it. Patience is normally defined as holding your tongue, and that is a fair description of one-half of patience. But the other half is equally important, and that is to loosen your tongue. Sometimes patience requires keeping your mouth closed. But other times it requires that you speak out.

In the short run, covering up aggravations, papering over differences, pretending that everything is well is relatively easy—much easier than trotting a problem out into the open and talking about it. In the long run, covering up and papering over is an exercise in impatience, in fact, because it means we lack the patience and restraint, the self-confidence and the self-control, the love and affection to be able to discuss, more or less rationally, more or less calmly, more or less civilly, those things which threaten our family happiness and love.

Oftentimes the holy family of Jesus, Mary and Joseph is described in such a way that we would be inclined to think of them as three doormats, holding their tongues, swallowing their emotions, putting up with aggravation, and equating patience with repression of honest emotions. Yet, if we stop to think about it, the holy family could hardly have been like that. Jesus, Mary and Joseph were all strong, vigorous, dynamic personalities. They simply could not, would not, and should not have gone around with hands folded, eyes downcast, talking to each other in pious and devout whispers —like we sometimes imagine life to be in religious communities. We have only two examples of conversation among the members of the holy family and they are heavily overlaid with theological reflection and religious teaching. But those who were much closer in time to the holy family than we are had no trouble describing the blunt dialogue between Jesus and Mary. Both in the temple at Jerusalem and at the marriage feast of Cana, Jesus and Mary spoke to each other candidly and confidently, unafraid to express their emotions and their feelings, and certainly not troubled by the thought that such honest exchanges threatened their deep affection or manifested impatience. On the contrary, one could argue that the dialogue in the temple and at Cana are excellent models of what patience really ought to be: two people speaking calmly, confidently, and affectionately, exchanging with one another differences of perception, differences of understanding, differences of experience. And then, quite clearly from the context of the story, their lives are deepened and enriched precisely because of their exchange.

In discussing the Holy Family it is customary to extol family virtues. Unfortunately, such family virtues often seem either creepy or impossible. Rarely do they include such essential attributes of a family relationship as openness, candor, honesty, courage, and confidence in the strength of the love of a relationship which enables people to take the routine chance of saying in effect, "Hey, I don't know what's going on, but I'm not sure I like it. Why don't we talk about it?"

In every intimate relationship, particularly between the husband and the wife, the normal state of things is that only rather small parts of the spectrum of the relationship are open for free and easy discussion. Other aspects of the relationship are raised only at the risk of one or the other partner blowing up. And yet other aspects, often most of the relationship, are by common consent ruled out of order, never to be thought about, never to be mentioned, never to be hinted at. Such mutually agreed upon hidden agendas are absolutely deadly for love; and unless and until intimate role partners can acquire the patience and the perseverance to have ALL dimensions of their relationship open for confident and candid discussion, then the combustibles pile up in the basement. One must truly say that candor is one of the most important, if not the most important, virtue to practice in family relationships, and especially in marriage—not the candor of the explosive blowup, but rather the loving candor that deals with problems long before the torch is put to the rags in the basement.

(Luke 2:41-52)

Too weary to care

THE Magi were patently mad. They left family and friends, home and occupation, a world they knew to journey over mountains, through dangerous badlands, and over deserts in pursuit of a star which they insisted heralded the advent of a very great king.

Surely there were Magi ("astrologers" would be another name for them) who disagreed with their interpretation of the star and who gave it a very different explanation. Surely there must have been grumblings and complaints from their families and considerable heartache when it came time for them to leave. And they must have wondered very often on that long and elusive trip whether it was worth the effort. Then the star disappeared and they came to a strange land with an odd king who consulted a rather unusual religious book and with a crafty look in his eyes sent them to a small town a few miles outside his capital city. They found no palace, no grandeur to indicate royalty—only a tiny house, a peasant couple, and a quite ordinary baby boy. Or so it seemed. But their calculations were precise. This little child over whom the star had risen could not be ordinary at all. So they left their gold, their frankincense and myrrh and went home, doubtlessly enormously satisfied that they had not failed in their quest. But why had they searched out the boy king? The answer was the same as that of all explorers down through human history: They searched him out because they knew he was there.

The point of the magi story is that Jesus came not just

for one race of people but for all nations, not just for one social class but for all social classes. He came for Jew and Gentile, wiseman and shepherd, intellectual and peasant, Greek and Roman, black and white, slave and free. In one time and at one place and very much a part of his own culture, environment, and milieu, he was a gift for all humankind; and the gold, frankincense and myrrh that the Magi brought were gifts in response. But if Jesus came for all, no matter what their race, creed, nationality, or socioeconomic status, he came only for those who search, for those who persist, for those who will not quit or give up, for those who will seek him out no matter how weary, discouraged, or frustrated they might feel. The search for Jesus is something like a treasure hunt; we, too, must find our way to Bethlehem, and it is a tricky, difficult route. We will never get there if we give up too soon.

If we grow weary and discouraged with the challenges and difficulties and frustrations of life, we forget that life without challenge, life without excitement, life without trial and difficulty would be even worse. Challenges may be exhausting, but boredom destroys everything that is human within us. The happiness and the fulfillment, the joy that we are always looking for in life and which always seems to elude us should be drawing us toward Jesus. We will probably only find him completely and totally at the end of our life, but the more we realize that the God who is revealed to us through the child at Bethlehem is the God for whom we search, the God for whom we climb mountains and traverse valleys. When we seek wealth, power, prestige and pleasure and when we love well or not well, when we experience frustration and discouragement in our search for happiness and joy in this world, it is all intended to challenge us and to call forth from us the best that is in us, to bring out of the depths of our personalities our courage and our dedication. All of us are born adventurers, romantics, searchers, explorers. The dull, prosaic business of life that squeezes the love of adventure out of most of us should turn us toward religion, which is designed to turn us into magi, the people who took the risk of crossing the desert because a star shone over a newborn babe. Religion is not supposed to make life dull; it is supposed to make it exciting. When religion does seem dull, monotonous, routine, and boring, there is something wrong with the religion or our perception of it.

The star must have exploded with dazzling brightness in the night sky. Perhaps, in modern terms, it was a supernova. It shook the Magi out of the routine of their ordinary life and demanded that they seek the cause of the dazzling new star. It was for them a religious experience, something that shattered their ordinary perceptions and gave them a new way of looking at life. So it should be also with us. We should seek the babe at Bethlehem to stir us out of the routine and the monotony of the winter months, to turn us from plodders to searchers, from dullards to adventurers, from cynics to romantics, hardened realists to men and women of dreams and missions.

(Matthew 2:1-12)

A question of love

ONCE there was a boy who was away at school and terribly in love with a girl who lived in his neighborhood. He was busy studying for exams; so was she. They agreed, especially since her parents wouldn't pay the phone bill any more, that they would stop calling one another and write letters every day instead. So the boy wrote his letter every evening and dropped it in the mailbox every morning on his way to class. He didn't hear a word from the girl. Days went by, then weeks, and then a whole month. He stopped writing because he was very, very angry. She had said she loved him, but obviously she didn't, because if she had loved him, wouldn't she have answered his letters? When he came home at vacation, the girl wouldn't speak to him on the telephone. Her friends said she was furious with him and looking for a new boyfriend. The young man was about ready to die. Then his mother said, "Hey, did you tell your girlfriend that you changed your post office box number at school?" "Well?"

There is no love story entirely free of complications. In fact, if we read a story in which the course of true love is absolutely smooth and serene, we quickly lose interest because we know there are always complications, misunderstandings, reversals, troubles. Boy meets girl is appealing only when boy loses girl (or girl loses boy) and then finds her (or him) again. Happy endings are only happy when we have to struggle for them. We know from experience that even the most powerful and passionate of loves is affected by misunderstandings, doubts, conflicts, problems—sometimes as silly as forgetting to change a post office box number, sometimes as profound and painful as a bitter disagreement.

We can best understand the gospel story of "doubting" Thomas if we understand it not as a story of intellectual doubt but a doubt about love. Thomas, obviously, was not sitting back with calm dispassion, considering the ultimate meaning of love and wondering what meaning life had if Jesus who was dead was indeed alive again. Thomas did not doubt God's capacity to bring Jesus back to life; Thomas rather doubted that God had enough love for both Jesus and Thomas to bring Jesus back to life.

We only begin to understand the passion and the power of the Thomas drama when we understand that it is a question of love. Thomas had lost his confidence in God's love. He no longer trusted God's love. He was exactly in the same position as the young lover who waits for the mail to bring a letter from his beloved only to be disappointed when no letter comes. The next step is to doubt the lover and to doubt the love and to wonder whether the mail will ever bring a letter. God had revealed his love through Jesus, or so it appeared, and then he had taken Jesus away and there was no more message from God or Jesus in the daily mail. Thomas, who had begun to believe that God really loved him, was now forced to the reluctant conclusion that God didn't love him after all. He had become reluctant to believe again because he didn't want to become vulnerable again. His reaction when the evidence of God's continued love was too overpowering to doubt any more, was the reaction of any lover overwhelmed by the persistence and fidelity of his or her beloved revealed and renewed once again.

There are such things in life as intellectual doubt; and there are some people who can overcome such doubt by philosophical argument; and it is a useful part of our education to consider such doubt and to listen to the philosophical arguments. But most of what passes in life for religious doubt is something more than just intellectual. Doubt is rather a profound questioning of whether there is goodness and love in the world. The doubter sees all the evil that occurs and all the suffering and misery. And then he may say, "I have an intellectual problem about the existence of God." In fact he means, "I simply do not believe in Love, if all these terrible things can happen. For surely God could have arranged things better, and surely God could have sent us more powerful evidences of love. Therefore, I doubt, I distrust, I refuse to risk myself by being open and vulnerable to a universe filled with ugly absurdity. There is no love."

So the doubter is normally not someone with just an intellectual problem. The doubter is someone who does not believe that he is loved. Indeed, all of us are doubters some of the time, perhaps a good deal of the time. We doubt we are loved and we doubt God's love. We may masquerade these doubts as propositional and cognitive; but in fact they are deeply emotional and affect the total personality. The doubter in each one of us, like doubting Thomas in today's gospel, is lonely, cut off, isolated, not wanted, unloved. There are, of course, signs that God loves us. In fact, from God's point of view it may even be argued that the signs are overwhelming that he has filled the world with so many good things for us. But he has also permitted bad things to exist in the world, and it is these bad things that shake our confidence in the good things. The evidence of the possibility of love is there, in other words, but we lack certainty that God may be revealing himself and his passionate concern for us especially in our human love.

If we take our love relationships as revelational, then we have to be content with the certainty that comes only after we say, "My Lord and my God" (another way to say the same thing would be, "I do believe you love me"). In the act of committing ourselves we acquire certainty that we are loved, though it always needs to be renewed. That's all there can be for the doubting Thomas that lurks in the frightened, lonely, alienated part of the personality of each of us. Faith does not preceed the act of love, in other words; it rather comes after. We make the enormous leap of trust in our beloved and then realize that because we love we also believe.

(John 20:19-31)

Searching for security

THE great basketball star, Doctor J., was fooling around on a neighborhood basketball court one day, practicing dunk shots from every angle around the basket, throwing in left-handed hook shots from twenty feet, right-handed hook shots from thirty feet, and flipping the ball from left hand to right as he made lay-ups off the backboard. A little girl, about nine years old, was watching Dr. J. very solemnly and very closely. Finally, he said to her, "What do you want, little girl?" "I can beat you in a game of horse," she said. "Don't be silly, little girl," Dr. J. replied; "nobody can beat the Doctor when it comes to horse." "I can," she said. "All right," said Dr. J., "let's play." To his horror, the little girl beat him H-O-R-S-E to 0. And Dr. J. went home and said to his wife, "I want three aspirin, absolute silence in the house, and a long, long nap."

The above is not a true story, but you can imagine how put down any great basketball player would be if a little child were to make him look ridiculous on the basketball court. That's how Simon Peter felt about Jesus. For if Simon Peter wasn't the finest fisherman on the lake, we know enough about his personality from the gospel stories to know that he thought he was. He knew fishing backwards, forwards, up and down, in and out. He understood the current, the temperatures, the wind, and the eating habits of the fish. There was no one who knew more about fishing than Peter. And who was Jesus? Well, he was a carpenter from up in the hills. Now, he may have been a good carpenter but carpenters don't know beans about fishing. Yet every time he went out on the lake it seemed that Peter never caught any fish until Jesus told him where to drop the net. As you can imagine, that really irked Peter no end. After awhile, as Father John Shea has jokingly suggested, Peter began to suspect that Jesus put one finger in the lake and made the fish go away, then later on, he put another finger in the lake and made the fish come back. Jesus might be a great rabbi, a marvelous preacher of Good News and a wonderful storyteller, but how could he know more about fishing than Simon, the son of John? It simply wasn't fair.

So after the resurrection when Peter encountered a stranger on the shore who seemed to know exactly where the fish were when Peter and his colleagues had not been able to make a single catch all night long, it was pretty clear to Peter who the stranger was and what he wanted. Peter had gone out in the boat to catch fish and Jesus came to the shore to catch Peter. This time Peter knew he was finished. For all his life he had been confident of his own ability to handle any situation. After all, was he not the best fisherman on the lake, and couldn't he cope in awkward and difficult situations? Peter knew his way around; he knew he could take care of himself. Now, however, he had encountered power and love so overwhelming that he could no longer take care of himself. He could no longer cope. He had discovered that it was both impossible and unnecessary to cope.

Our lives are shaky, contingent, uncertain, fragile affairs. We hang poised, so it seems, between two oblivions. We can be snuffed out any instant by an automobile accident, a fire, a virus, by nuclear explosion. We can be abandoned by family, friends, those we love who are themselves precarious, iffy beings. Therefore we try to build up for ourselves a base which would be at least temporarily secure and from which we could defend ourselves and fight off the rest of the world. From this base we are at least masters of our own fate, directors of our own destiny, controllers of our own life. For Peter it was his skill as a fisherman; for each of us it may be our career success, our aggressiveness or our reservation, our caution, money—whatever, we all have something that plays the role in our life that fishing played in Peter's. Here, at least, we are in charge. And Jesus dissolves the walls around Peter's fortress with a flick of the finger, a word. Peter's fishing skills are trivial, unimportant. Even at fishing Jesus and the loving Father whom he represents are infinitely better.

"Give it up," is what Jesus says to Peter and through Peter to us. Security is not to be found in skill or career or defense mechanisms or power, wealth, or pleasure. For Peter, the challenge was not to give up his skills as a fisherman and trust that every time he went into the lake Jesus would automatically show up and point out where the fish were. The challenge, rather, is to put our trust not in our own skills or ability to protect ourselves but where it belongs—in God's passionate, providing love which has been revealed to us through Jesus. In a way it would be easier to depend on God for everything or depend on God for nothing. In the latter case our own abilities would be all important; in the former we wouldn't need abilities. But God chooses to treat us like equals, demanding that we do our part to the best of our

115

abilities and leave the rest to him. To "leave the rest to him" comes hard, but this injunction is the core of the Easter message. Even when we have fished all night and accomplished nothing we should not be afraid or disheartened or despairing, for Jesus waits on the shore.

(John 21:1-19)

A friend no matter what

THREE young men owned an establishment licensed by the state to serve liquor to the public. They were minding their own business when three "toughs" entered the establishment and took immediate exception to the expression on the face of one of the young owners. As it happens, one word led to another and there were some blows exchanged, some breakage of material, and the lights suddenly went out. When one of the young toughs regained consciousness, the establishment was both demolished and empty. "What happened to my friends?" he demanded. The next day, when his "friends" visited him in the hospital, he asked them the same question. "Well," said one, "after the lights went out we didn't think we could help, so we kind of left." "You're no friends of mine," said the young man; "anyone who won't stick around when the lights go out certainly doesn't care what happens to me."

Friends are almost by definition people you can count on no matter what. You may be close to others; there may be things you have in common with others that you don't share with a friend. You and your friend may quarrel, you may even not speak to one another. You may disagree over politics, religion, art, food, athletic teams—all those important issues in life; but nonetheless he or she is still a friend precisely because when you need one, he or she is there. You can count on a friend when the lights go out, when the chips are down, when the going gets tough, when everyone else deserts

117

you, and when there's nothing for anyone to gain by standing by you. Then you know who is your friend and who isn't.

The Kingdom of Heaven, the Good News which Jesus came to preach, in essence involves a relationship, indeed a relationship of enormous intimacy between God and humankind. Jesus himself, who preached the Kingdom of Heaven, also revealed it in his own intimacy with God. So there is no fundamental contradiction between our hailing Jesus as the Son of God and our hailing the Kingdom of Heaven, since Jesus symbolizes, embodies, incarnates and makes real to all of us this relationship between God and humanity. Note well, however, that the Kingdom of Heaven does not add something to a situation where there was nothing before. God was already present in loving unity with humankind before the coming of Jesus. Jesus merely revealed the depth and the breadth of this unity; he showed to us how much there is of God in us already by preaching his Father's love for us and also by incarnating the Father in himself, becoming the absolute and the ultimate sacrament of that unity, that intimacy, between God and humankind.

All human intimacies become legitimate images, symbols, and sacraments of God's intimacy with us because each of them reveals something about that intimacy. Saints and theologians through the centuries have been quite dramatic in the kinds of human relationship they have used to illustrate the intimacy between God and us. So God (and Jesus) has been described as mother, father, brother, sister, nurse, friend, lover, knight. Anselm of Canterbury, the great early medieval theologian and saint, referred to Jesus as a mother and a nurse because he gives us life and he sustains our life with his nourishment. It is in this context that the Kingdom of Heaven involves relationship, and all human relationships reveal something about this relationship. The Good Shepherd image—the shepherd knows his sheep and the sheep know the shepherd—is perhaps the one that most heavily emphasizes intimacy. In the different gospel stories the shepherd is depicted either as a protector of his sheep or the one who searches for lost sheep, or the one who herds all the sheep together. While the Good Shepherd symbol can have many different, though related, meanings (like all symbols), at the core of each of the various interpretations is the notion of friendship and intimacy. The shepherd and the sheep are on the closest and most intimate of terms. With the Good Shepherd we celebrate the intimacy of our relationship with Jesus, the fact that Jesus is the kind of friend who will never desert us no matter how bad the situation and no matter how dark it may be when the lights go out, no matter how alone and defenseless we may seem to be.

As we have noted many times, the essence of the Good News of the Kingdom is love and power. God loves us and wills to take care of us and has the power to take care of us. It is a reasurance we can't hear too often, because we are fundamentally suspicious and distrustful. Why should God bother to love us, and, if he does, does he really have the power to protect us, if not from the trials and tribulations of everyday life, then at least from eternal obliteration? The Good Shepherd story is the response of Jesus to those questions. For us the issue, as always, is whether we are willing to believe Jesus.

(John 10: 27-30)

Being in love is hard work

ONCE there was a man and a woman who had been married for almost thirty years. It was a so-so marriage —some love, some anger, and, as the years went by, a considerable amount of habit and indifference. Then the woman, who hadn't been feeling well, was told by her doctor that she had only a year to live. She told her husband then how much she cared for him and how much she couldn't stand him at the same time. He responded in kind, and they had a bitter quarrel. After the quarreling was over, however (and it lasted only for a coule of days), they began to really love each other, as if for the very first time. And the year's time that was left to them was the happiest in their lives, happier than all the others put together. "If only we had known sooner," said her husband the day she was buried.

The words, "Little children, love one another," are as unassailable as Mother's Day cards, Fourth of July oratory, and Christmas trees. Nobody is against it. However, when anything becomes so much a part of Established Truth it becomes trite, pretty, and irrelevant. Nobody listens to what it really means or reflects on its challenges. Love is sweet, love is romance, love is pleasant, love happens in June, which rhymes with moon. So we who are like children before the Lord Jesus, in other words, should feel sweet, pleasant, and kindly toward one another.

In fact, love is terribly hard work and can only be sustained with the maximum of effort, honesty, candor, courage, and resourcefulness. Even the sexual dimension of love, based as it is on extremely powerful needs and rewarded with enormous physical pleasure, can be sustained only with difficulty. The two partners have to work hard at understanding each other's needs, moods, vulnerabilities, and defences, fears and hopes in the physical dimensions of their relationship. Since the self-discipline required in exercising such sensitivity and openness are too much for many people, the physical aspects of love normally deteriorate very quickly (according to statistics, particularly after the first two years of marriage).

In many, if not most, relationships, once the physical passions and pleasures have been permitted to deteriorate, the other components of the relationship decline rapidly, because the motivation for their sustenance is much less powerful. The fully and completely human dimensions of a love relationship require (normally) the fuel of passion to keep the engine running. However, if the two humans are not working at the discipline, the self-restraint, the sensitivity, the capacity to comfort and challenge in all the dimensions of their common life, then the fuel tanks of passion will dry up very quickly. Intimacy with another person, even intimacy reinforced by sexual passion, is perhaps the most difficult challenge in life, a challenge which many people do not understand and which others pretend does not exist and still others ignore because the openness, vulnerability and love involved are too terrifying.

When Jesus told us to love one another even as he has loved us, he presented us with an extraordinarily difficult, indeed, almost impossible, challenge. It is not pretty, it is not sentimental, it is not saccharine sweet; rather it is terrifying, awesome, almost impossible.

Perhaps the most difficult part of intimacy is that we have to take risks. We have to expose ourselves, we might have to put the relationship in jeopardy. And while we can be moderately confident (particularly if our habits of sensitivity and intimacy have been developed through practice) that new exposure of oneself will help the relationship to grow, we can never be absolutely certain. Tough and honest talk, painful self-revelation (which are not the same thing, incidentally, as using the latest fashionable psychological terminology for purposes of exploiting and manipulating the other) can be frightening exercises. If they are successful, the rewards are great; if they fail, the pain can be horrible. And, of course, some of the time they do fail. The ultimate risk of intimacy comes when, having balanced off the successes and failures, we resolve that there are some grounds for trying again, modest reasons for hope and optimism.

The love that Jesus has for us is not merely a model for such risk-taking. Look how much he revealed of himself and put himself in jeopardy for us. It was also, and equally important, a motive and a guarantee. Jesus does not promise that we will not be hurt in our human intimacy; he does not even promise that we will always be successful. He does promise to continue to love us no matter what happens, and that he will sustain that love no matter how may times someone breaks our hearts.

(John 13:31-33, 34-35)

Boring, boring, boring

A CERTAIN man and woman worked hard all their lives and raised a large family while all the time they managed to juggle separate careers. They were busy, busy all the time, running, rushing, never enjoying any peace. They promised themselves that they would retire early and catch up on the peace and relaxation they had been deprived of all their married life. They would read, he would tend the garden and organize his stamp collection, she would take pictures and jog. They would be content to spend the rest of their lives together in relaxation and peace. So they retired and moved to a place where it was sunny most of the time and busied themselves with gardens and photographs, jogging and reading. Then, finally, after about three weeks of this paradise existence, they were sitting relaxed by the edge of the pool, and the husband said to his wife, "You know what?" She said, "You're bored." And he said, "You, too, huh?"

It was something like this Jesus had in mind when he said he was going to leave us peace, but not as the world meant peace. This statement is perfectly compatible with something else he said about his coming not to bring peace but the sword. For the peace which Jesus brings often seems like the sword. He did not promise us a life of effortless ease, of serene relaxation, quiet solitude, of restful comfort. Rather the peace that Jesus came to bring was a peace that involved action, challenge, effort, suffering, risk-taking. The peace that Jesus promised was not the peace of inaction but one of commitment, purpose, of being swept up in something exciting and important.

It is the only peace, however, that human beings really want. We may think that all we want is to be left alone, that we will be happy if the world goes away and forgets about us, if the telephone and the doorbell don't ring and there is nothing to do of an evening but sit and relax. It is surely true that some of us rush too much and become massive, shambling blobs of fretful anxiety. The answer to that, however, is not total inactivity but peaceful action in which we respond to the challenges of life and let God worry about the outcome. Those who at various times in Christian history fled to the monasteries to escape from the world soon discovered that even in the monastic life tensions and conflicts of the world followed. Peace does not come from escape but from calm and confident response. There is no peace, in other words, this side of paradise. And even in paradise peace will much more likely come from intense action rather than from complete inaction.

There is an analogy between personal peace and world peace. Some people seem to think that all we have to do is to lay down arms and there will be peace, that if we run from the turmoil of a confused and challenging world order, then that world order will change. The hard work of patient, sustained negotiation is not needed, they tell us; peace is a simple matter of escape, not complicated at all. World peace, like personal peace, is perilous; it requires courage, it is defeated by recklessness which some people confuse with courage.

125

Andrew M. Greeley

Whether in our personal lives or in the lives of the world's people, the biggest temptation is weariness. Must we keep on every day responding to challenges? Will not the challenges go away, at least for a time—summer vacation, perhaps, after the kids are grown up and out of the house, or when we retire? Is it not possible that then the challenges will diminish, the demands will pass, and we can sit back and enjoy and relax? The answer is no; enjoyment and relaxation come in the midst of challenge and not after it's over. If one takes challenge out of life the result is not peace but boredom.

(John 14:23-29)

The pain of ingratitude

IT happened that a man asked another man to lend him $500. The man who asked for the loan desperately needed the money, and the man who made the loan had scraped together every last cent he had. But a very good friend was in desperate need and the lender thought that when your friends were in trouble you helped when you could. So he made the loan and was promised it would all be paid back in regular installments within a year. As it happened, he never received a penny back and his friend stopped talking to him, avoided him on every occasion, and even began spreading nasty stories about him behind his back. When he finally made lots of money he never even remembered the loan. "No good deed ever goes unpunished."

During the Last Supper Jesus prayed not that his followers be taken away from the world's resentments and envy but rather that they live in the world and be protected from such resentments and envy. Sometimes, particularly when we were in school, we were given the impression that the "world" from which Jesus was praying for protection was full of temptations, particularly temptations to sins of the "flesh." But clearly this is not what Jesus had in mind. Nor is it what John had in mind when writing to a beleaguered, presecuted and resented early Christian community. The "world" which was making life difficult for John's readers was represented by some Jewish leaders who had the Christians expelled from the synagogue—a terrible punishment, since at that time the people in John's community were mostly Jews who considered themselves part of the Jewish community. They were horrified at being excluded from the synagogue—as we would be if a pastor should exclude us from entering the church in a parish where we had lived all our lives. The world was also represented by the Roman government which had heard vicious, nasty rumors about the Christians and was beginning to make life difficult for them politically. (Much of the persecution in the early church was based on slander. The accusations brought against the early Christians—like those brought against Jesus—were false, a point often overlooked in the Christian glorification of martyrs.)

Resentment, envy and the punishment of generosity and good deeds are some of the most unattractive and horrifying components of the human personality. Yet those unfortunate few who seem quite incapable of such emotions are often the prime targets of other people's envy and resentments. Jesus prayed in the gospel we read today that his followers be protected from the terrors stirred up by snide and resentful viciousness. But if we all examine our conscience closely, we will discover that oftentimes we are on the side of the "world," and we are the ones who persecute the good, the talented, the successful, the generous. We go after the fellow student who works hard, the friend who is terribly attractive, the coworker who seems successful, the spouse or the child who wins more praise than we do, the person who helps us in time of need or difficulty. We do everything we can to punish those who for reasons of dedication or generosity or maybe just plain natural gifts are the followers of Jesus.

When Life Hurts

Why do we punish those who do good deeds? Why did some Jewish leaders and some Roman politicans go after the early Christians who were harmless and inoffensive people? Why did the leaders in Jerusalem seek to destroy Jesus, who in fact was no threat to their spiritual and temporal worlds? Why did the man in our opening story punish the friend who helped him out when he needed money? Why do we so profoundly and bitterly resent goodness, and why do we feel such a compelling need to destroy the good man or woman? Why does that need, in some acute cases of envy, lead to actual assassinations? And why, in many cases where we stop short of physical murder, do we not hesitate to commit moral, emotional or psychological murder? The answer seems to be twofold: (1) We envy those who are good because their goodness seems to deprive us of something that is rightfully ours, and (2) we punish them because their goodness is somehow a judgment of our mediocrity and our nastiness.

Jesus was executed by the "world" because his life was an affront to religious leaders who were not popular when he was and because his goodness was a challenge to anyone who knew him to be as good as he was. A person like that automatically writes his own death warrant. The early Christian community to which John was writing was thrown out of the synagogue by the Jews and persecuted by the Romans not because it violated either Roman or Jewish law but because its popularity and goodness threatened both church and state. So it has been with many of the saints down through the ages. They have been imprisoned, tortured, persecuted, denounced, and destroyed not by the outside "world" but by the members of their own church and communities. Because of their goodness and their popularity they become enormous threats to those who feel themselves (usually quite correctly) to be unattractive and mediocre.

Normally, the lesson that is drawn from the gospel is that the follower of Jesus must expect to be persecuted. Indeed, there are still places in the world today where Catholics are persecuted for their faith. But a more appropriate and more poignant lesson would be that those of us who claim to be followers of Jesus would be in the front of the crowd crying, "Crucify him! Crucify him!" if we encountered somebody who took the teachings of Jesus with full seriousness and hence was totally generous and performed all kinds of good deeds. We may claim in our words to be followers of Jesus, but, alas, in fact we are often punishers of good deeds.

(John 17:20-26)

But they are not like us

THERE once was a certain neighborhood where many ethnic groups lived in harmony: Poles, Irish, Italians, Germans, Swedes, French, English, even some Latvians and Lithuanians. They all got along fine with one another, they all celebrated each other's festivals, went to each other's pageants, and prodigiously consumed each other's food. But then some new ethnic groups moved in: Koreans, Filippinos, and Vietnamese. The crime rate didn't go up and the property values didn't go down (most of these new people were of the same financial status as the older residents) but the people of the neighborhood became worried: if one Vietnamese family moved onto the block, the whole block would turn. So they got together and said, "This has got to stop. We have a nice neighborhood the way it is and we just can't handle any more diversity."

When we read of the Pentecost experience in the gospel we should consider it against a background of the tower of Babel story from the book of Genesis. Luke clearly had this Babel "model" in mind and viewed the Pentecost experience of wind and fire and tongues as "canceling out" what happened at Babel. For when humankind, in its pride, tried to build a tower to heaven, then the languages were confused and disunity followed. But when God, in his love, sent the Holy Spirit, people with different tongues heard the same story. The Babel story is one of conflict created by pride while the Pentecost story is one of unity created by love. The Babel story was a religious (not scientific or historical) explanation of the conflicts which human sinfulness produced among nations and peoples. Pride and arrogance led to contentiousness and diversity.

We must note, however, that Luke's approach does not eliminate the diversity; it only eliminates the negative effect that human sinfulness creates out of diversity. The Parthians, the Medes, the Elamites, the Pontians, and the Capadocians also continued to be diverse people with different tongues and cultures. Each of them hears the followers of Jesus talking in his own tongue. Babel is not undone by the elimination of different languages but rather by the appearance of a gospel that can be understood in every language. Diversity will persist but it will not be made destructive by human sinfulness. On the contrary, it will be integrated into a gospel that preaches love for all. Christianity will not demand of the Parthians, the Medes, the Elamites, the Pontians, and the Capadocians or the inhabitants of Libya about Cyrene that they give up their language, their customs, or their cultures. Neither will it demand the same thing of the Poles, the Irish, the Italians, the Swedes, or the Koreans, the Filippinos, the Chinese, the Vietnamese, or the Indians. On the contrary, Christians will absorb and celebrate the riches of every cultural tradition precisely because everything that is true, good and beautiful is already Christian and need not be feared. Diversity is to be celebrated.

Any Christian attempt to equate the gospel with one culture (as did the Renaissance popes who banned the Jesuit experiments in India and China, which cost the Church the whole Asian continent, and the Western missionaries who expected Chinese converts to become

Westerners) do horrendous violence to the Christian tradition. The continental missionaries who swarmed into Ireland in the 400s and 500s A.D. took over that pagan culture almost entirely. The so-called Celtic cross, which was a pagan fertility symbol, was said to stand for Jesus and Mary; the Brigid cross, which was the sun symbol, stood for Christ the light of the world; the shrines, the holy places and even the saints of pagan Ireland became shrines, holy places and saints of Christian Ireland. If it was good and true, if it could help people's lives, then, of course, it was Christian. The genius of the gospel is all inclusive.

Pentecost, then, is the celebration of unity that is achieved by the integration of and celebration of diversity and not by the imposition of uniformity. Pentecost is a Christian feast of cultural pluralism. Christians celebrate the riches of cultural variety that abound in the world. But while the genius of Christianity has always been pluralist, it is sadly true that many of us Christians are narrow uniformists who want everyone to be like us and who desire to impose a cultural, linguistic and religious straightjacket on all the followers of the Lord Jesus. We think the customs associated with the faith of other people—the Hispanic love of festivals and parties, the Polish propensity to make bread every time there is a religious feast, the Italian custom of having bands at funerals, the different styles of grief displayed by various ethnic groups—not only unusual and strange, but alarming, threatening and intolerable. Moreover, in the post-Vatican church the many different styles of Catholicism that have emerged deeply disturb us. There is only one way to be a good Catholic, and that is our way —whether it be charismatic or Opus Dei or liberation theology or marriage encounter or Genesis II or whatever, it has to be done our way and our way only. Anyone who does not do it our way is not only depriving himself or herself, but is also likely to be wrong and morally and religiously deficient. Indeed, it is not unknown for those who make special claims of following the inspirations of a pentecostal spirit to be utterly intolerant of the diversity which in Luke's story shows the Spirit coming to validate, reinforce and celebrate.

Let us be honest about it. That which is different, strange or unusual often is threatening. We have to make a major effort not to condemn or denounce but rather to understand, to appreciate, to enjoy. It takes self-discipline and restraint to realize that diversity is not the result of sinfulness but the result of God's superabundant creativity, and that those who are different from us, even if they do play their stereos at peak volume or yell out family squabbles at the top of their lungs, are not necessarily inferior, wrong, evil, malicious, or "foreign devils" for behaving that way. They are just different. We may prefer our customs, but if we are truly pluralistic, truly Christian, we may be able to see that there are certain advantages in their customs too. The Spirit at Pentecost reminds us that within the kingdom of the faith there are many mansions, and within the household of the faith on this earth there is room for the others as well as for us.

(Acts 2:1-11)

Trying too hard

IT seems like such a long time ago since Joe Namath played quarterback. Occasionally he was called "Broadway Joe." He played football for the New York Jets. He had wobbly legs, a wide mouth, and a golden arm, and, if the newspapers are to be believed, an incorrigible propensity to party. One year Broadway Joe's Jets made it to the Superbowl. They were heavy underdogs. The other team was good in every respect: they were serious and sober young men; they practiced hard, studied their game plan, and went to bed before curfew every night. Broadway Joe talked and partied and assured every reporter he could find that the Jets would roll over their opposition. By Super Sunday every football fan in the country, save for the fans of the New York Jets, wanted to see the ball rammed down Broadway Joe's loud mouth. He wasn't taking the game seriously; he was turning the solemn ritual of Super Sunday into a farce; he deserved to lose the game to the serious, sober, dedicated young men on the other team. The rest is history. Broadway Joe had a field day and the Jets won the Superbowl. He who saves his life shall lose it and he who loses his life shall save it.

There is a story of an "identity crisis" in the gospel, not indeed that Jesus was in doubt about his own identity but rather a crisis his contemporaries felt. In the gospel Jesus answers the question of his identity by saying that he is the one who carries the cross and attracts followers who will do the same. He is the one who by losing his life shall save it and show his followers how by losing their lives they can save them. People who were having an identity crisis over Jesus demanded that he tell them whether he was the Messiah or king or a political, revolutionary leader. Jesus simply ignored the thrust of the questions and described those potential identities as irrelevant. He was, he said, in effect the Suffering Servant from the book of Isaiah, the one who carries the cross, the one who loses his life and thus saves it. This opaque, mysterious and paradoxical answer baffled those who questioned Jesus. The pertinent question about Jesus was not who he was but what did he come to reveal. He came to reveal that only by trusting in the overwhelming power of God's love could one possibly save one's life.

We know from our own experience how it is "being loose" that wins and "being uptight" that loses. A good athletic team is poised, relaxed, and confident (though not overconfident). A losing team is uptight, rigid, awkward, and prone to foolish mistakes. The student does much better in a test when his attitude is one of "don't give a hoot" than of grim, do-or-die seriousness. A relaxed public speaker is far more effective than a nervous one. Success in life's important contests requires a certain amount of alertness and tension, but it also demands confidence, relaxation, a kind of carefree flair and joy. To be able to win the big one you have to be able to live gracefully with losing it. Then the contest is in its proper perspective and your energies and resources can be devoted to playing the game well and not be distracted by anxieties and fears. Franklin

Roosevelt was perfectly right when he said in 1933 that the only thing we had to fear was fear itself.

The truth of being ready psychologically to lose one's life in order to save it is a hint and a sacrament of an even more profound religious truth. We live well only when we are able to accept gracefully the fact of our own death and the pain of all the little deaths that are inevitable in the course of our lives. The uptight shall not inherit the earth; nor shall they inherit the Kingdom of Heaven. Though part of being uptight may be genetic, cultural, or psychological, part of it is also religious. Wherever we may be on the "uptight" scale, faith moves us up the scale toward loose and confident and hopeful and graceful (in the sense of full-of-hope and full-of-grace). The old Catholic saying that we work like everything depends on us and act like everything depends on God is true. After we do the best we can, we simply have to relax and trust in God. And if we approach the challenges of life hopefully and gracefully, then the part of responding to the challenge that depends on us can be done more smoothly, more effectively, and with greater flair and elegance. We are all afraid of losing our lives, but if we can contain that fear we shall find our life more effective in this world and rejoice in life for eternity with our friends, family, Jesus, and the heavenly Father.

Broadway Joe Namath had faith, perhaps not in God, but certainly in his wide receivers, his blockers, his ability to read the other team's defense, and in his own skill. He was a realist. He knew how good he was—good enough to beat the Baltimore Colts. Faith is finally no more than realism. As we face the challenges of life and death and rebirth we have faith in our confidence and a realistic appraisal not necessarily of our own abilities but of God's power and love.

(Luke 9:18-24)

Yearning for a home

IN the gospel Jesus tells us that he is homeless and promises homelessness for his followers. It is a grim and dismaying depiction of the Christian life with not even the prospect of having a home somewhere else. What does Jesus mean when he says he has no home? What is the homelessness that he promises us? For after all, Jesus did have his mother and his relatives in Nazareth, did have his band of followers, and wherever they went for the night must have been home of a sort. He also had his Father's home in heaven, and we who are Christians and disciples of Jesus have homes of our own with our families and friends. Are we to give these up? Is Jesus saying that we all should become solitaries living by ourselves in the desert with no home and no telephone line to home? What is the point in the comparison by contrast between the foxes having their nests and Jesus having no place in which to lay his head?

For some followers of Jesus, particularly for missionaries, the poetry of the "homeless" passage may have a direct and literal application. (Though with the coming of jet air travel, even the missionary is not that far from home.) To understand Jesus' reference to being without a home we must realize once again that Jesus was a storyteller. He used vivid imagery to illumine and excite the imaginations of those who listened to him. It is a major mistake to try to interpret with rigid literalness the free-flowing imagery and metaphor of the storyteller, especially because such interpretation usually misses and sometimes destroys the point. Jesus is talking about the loneliness of the follower of Jesus, the alienation that is inevitable for any Christian, the longing and the yearning that the Christian life is bound to create and not satisfy. Jesus is saying that this is like homelessness, and, in a way, perhaps even worse than homelessness. There are at least two different kinds of loneliness involved in the Christian life. And it would appear that Jesus may have had both in mind. The first yearning is the yearning for the fullness of God's love that Jesus has revealed to us, promised to us, yet not yet granted to us completely. "Our hearts are restless till they rest in thee," says St. Augustine. Mankind does have a hunger for the absolute, the ultimate, the perfect; and there is an inevitable restlessness about all human life as we search for the perfect love. Christianity, by telling us that this perfect love is possible and indeed waits for us increases the yearning and the loneliness by making it explicit and by tantalizing us with the promise that the love we half-hoped might exist does in fact exist and desires us and waits for us.

Moreover, and this is the second point that Jesus is making and probably the principal one he wishes to emphasize for his followers as they go out on their mission, to be a good Christian makes one something of an alien, something of an extraterrestrial among one's fellow human beings. The condition is not necessarily better or more virtuous or more generous than other human beings but it does mean that Christians live with a much more conscious awareness of the transient nature of our present existence. We Christians do believe and at least some of the time act as if there is a transcendent dimension to life that makes it possible for us to feel completely at home in the present phase of our lives. There are new heavens, new earths, new kingdoms, new adventures, new explorations. The Christian does not sink his or her roots quite so deeply or quite so blindly into this life as do those who do not believe in transcendence. Much of the abortion controversy, for example, is in fact a controversy over whether there is a transcendent dimension to life. Even some of the celibacy issue involves the belief in transcendence. For if you think this world is one's permanent and perhaps only home, then to give up the pleasures of sex and the joys of marriage is ridiculous. The attack on celibacy coincides with a swing away from the transcendental emphasis of Christianity in the direction of a secular emphasis. This swing, which happened in the 1960s, was necessary because some Christians had so emphasized the transcendent as to deny all value to the secular. Unfortunately, one extreme led to another.

In the last twenty years not a few Catholics seem to have so emphasized the secular as to destroy the transcendent, to have replaced one imbalance with another. Some of the anger to be found in certain attacks on celibacy can be easily understood as anger from those who do not think there is a home beyond our present home and are bitterly opposed to belief in an "outmoded" view of the universe. They want the Son of Man, in other words, to have a nest in this world like the foxes or the birds of the air. They do not want either the Son of Man or his priests to be homeless, to point in the direction of a world that is not only extraterrestrial but transcendental, a world which indeed includes the cosmos but goes far beyond it.

(Luke 9:51-62)

So much to do, so little time

THERE once was a mother who went on strike. She refused to wake up the children for school in the morning; she cooked no breakfasts; packed no lunches; washed no laundry; picked up no one after school to deliver to ballet, music or computer class; watched no hockey games; cooked no dinner; didn't settle fights after supper about what to watch on television. Nor did she harrass the children to do their homework. She lay in bed chewing on bonbons and laughed. The doctor who came to visit that evening said to the family, "She's not sick or crazy; she has just decided that there is so much work to be done in this house that it's impossible to begin. A perfectly sane reaction, it seems to me." (You see, the doctor was a woman and a mother too.)

Many of us, especially mothers, have had this experience. We are just so overwhelmed with work that we feel like giving up and not doing anything. What's the point in trying when you know that if you work hard all day you will only be further behind in the evening. It seems as though work makes things worse, not better. So why work? And nobody ever seems to be around to volunteer to help. If chaos will overcome order and miscreation wipe out creation, if the world is going to sink back into primal confusion, why fight it? Lie back and enjoy it.

Jesus must have felt this way when he lamented that the harvest was plentiful and the laborers so few. It was an expression that must have surprised those who heard him. The fields were probably ripe for harvest in Palestine and people were swarming through the fields picking the grain and putting it in baskets so that the food could be stored for the coming winter season when there would be nothing left to harvest. Virtually every available hand would be working in the fields during harvest time. But there was no shortage of workers because in an impoverished country like Palestine there was almost always less work than workers. Harvest time offered an opportunity to store up not only food for the winter but the resources necessary to purchase food and other things to keep families alive. The followers of Jesus and those who listened to his stories would have had a hard time imagining a situation in which there were not enough workers for the harvest.

Jesus was talking not about the grain harvest but about the spiritual harvest, about the desperate hunger for meaning in life, and a desperate need to be healed from the sickness of sin and guilt and hopelessness. There was so much to do, so many people to whom the Good News must be preached, so many troubled and worried persons to be comforted, so many busy and indifferent persons to be challenged. Jesus could not do it all himself, and that is why he drafted seventy-two followers and sent them on their brief missions to various towns in Palestine to act in his name, to bring truth, goodness, love, and health in the name of Jesus to those who desperately hungered for the nourishment Jesus had to give them.

Why couldn't he have done it himself? After all, he was God, wasn't he? Jesus was God revealing himself in human form and subject to the limitations of human nature. He could not be in two places at once, he could not appear personally at all times in history, he could not speak to anyone and everyone who ever lived. Dependence on the seventy-two disciples during his public life was a sign that the Good News, the healing love, the saving power of the kingdom of God as revealed in Jesus would be shared through human helpers. We are taught to walk, to speak, to read and write, to operate our computers by other human beings; it is only fitting and appropriate that we learn about God's love through other human beings. The harvest of human personalities, their response to knowledge, love and healing as revealed in Jesus, depends on human cooperation. There is so much to do, and God is going to do it all with our cooperation. He has resolved to be dependent on us. Indeed, figuratively speaking, God has said that if we don't cooperate, he will act just like the mother in the story: he will lie in bed and eat bonbons. While it is true that without him we can do nothing, it is also true that without us to help spread the gospel he can do nothing.

This does not mean that we go out and propagandize others, cornering people on buses and airplanes, haranguing them on street corners, using high-pressure sales techniques to bring them into the church (though perhaps at times there is room for those techniques). We reveal God's challenging and healing love not so much by the things we say, not by our arguments, our advertising, or the persistence and determination of our sales techniques; we reveal God's love by loving. We are, each one of us, God's sacrament, God's agent in revealing his love to others. We are the most effective agents, the most dazzling sacraments for those who know us best and who are the most likely to be the recipients of our affection. Where we fail to be sensitive, tender, demanding, exciting, then God is, as it were, bound and gagged, because one of the principal channels of his love has been cut off.

When Jesus says, in effect, that there is so much work to be done, what he is really saying is that there is so much love that is needed and so few people brave enough, determined enough, resourceful enough, and free enough to do that loving.

(Luke 10:1-10)

Hanging by a thread

PICTURE a very wealthy man: he had enormous power and influence in his society and was deeply loved by his wife and children. He was walking down the street in a quiet neighborhood on a peaceful, lovely summer day. He was feeling very secure and confident because everything in his life was in order and he had very little to worry about. Then three masked men emerged from behind a bush. One twisted his arm behind his back, another put a knife to his throat, and a third demanded his wallet, rings, and watch. "If you don't give them to us, we'll kill you, and we might do it anyway for fun," said one of the men. The wealthy man quickly handed over his possessions and fell to his knees, begging for his life. The three punks laughed and took off. When the squad car finally came the man was still on his knees sobbing with terror. His life, he realized, had hung by a thread.

Of course, all our lives hang by a thread. At any moment a drunken driver might swerve out of control and smash into our car or run us down on the sidewalk. A heart might finally quit in protest, a cell might run wild and cause a cancer, a bird might fly into a jet engine and down the plane, a germ or a virus might bring us a deadly disease, a leaky gas main might explode. We are poised precariously on the brink of not being. We are caught for a few brief seconds between the oblivion that came before and the oblivion that will come after.

At no time will our power, our affluence, our possessions, our influence eliminate this precarious position.

It can protect us a bit with better food, better health care, better security, by increasing our life expectancy; but it is no more than an instant, really. And nothing can protect us from sudden violent incidents in which the forces of irrationality overwhelm our protections and leave us naked to the powers of destruction. We know this in the depths of our soul whenever the subject is raised. Yet we still try to hide, to protect ourselves, to build up physical and psychological defenses, to ward off the effects of our contingency and our fragility. We never quite get away with it, but we never stop trying.

The Good News that Jesus preached was NOT a message that denied our vulnerability or our finitude, for Jesus himself was a vulnerable man, as fragile as we are. He was arrested by petty religious political bosses and executed as a sacrifice to envy and ambition. There were, as he himself noted, no twelve legions of angels there to protect him, only one poor pathetic person with a sword. The message and the person of Jesus do not tell us that our insecurities are mistaken; on the contrary, what happened to Jesus ought to make all of us live in even deeper terror. If a man who was authentically good can be so easily liquidated, what chance have we? The horrors of the holocaust, of Auschwitz and the other concentration camps, stagger the imagination. But what, finally, is unjust is not that millions of people die before their time, but that any of us die at all. Indeed, if life comes into existence only to be snuffed out so shortly, what is the point of it all?

So we have lots of insecurities, and they are justified. But the gospel of Jesus tells us that even though we cannot overcome our contingency and our vulnerability, even though we can't protect ourselves from the Ultimate Disaster, there are still grounds for hope, for confidence. We can find security of a sort, although it is a very different kind from what most of us want. We can find security in God's love, a love that is implacable, unshatterable, and irrevocable. It is a power so awesome that God has the strength to finally protect us, to validate his commitment of love to us. That is the essence of the gospel message. We can find security only in God's love. It is a security that does not eliminate our insecurity and vulnerability, but rather promises that it will validate itself beyond our limitations. Our contingency and vulnerability will not have the last word, death will not speak the final sentence. Precisely because of the power and the passion of God's love we shall survive no matter what happens. The tears will be wiped away and there will be only joy, happiness, and peace. That is what the gospel is all about, and if it doesn't mean that, it means nothing at all. For us the challenge of faith is whether we really do believe in the passionate power of God's love, a love which will validate God's commitment to us just as it validated his commitment to Jesus in the resurrection. The faith issue, then, is very simple: Does God love us enough and is God powerful enough to protect us from destruction?

(Luke 12:13-21)

Humility is not self-deprecation

THE eighth-grade girl who had the lead in her school play ("West Side Story") practiced very hard learning her lines, singing her songs, working on her dance steps. Her family was very proud that she had the lead and they all encouraged her. Indeed, they encouraged her so vigorously that they wouldn't give her any time to relax. A whole week before the play was to be performed she had the role of Maria down perfectly. But her parents kept pushing because they were afraid she might mess up one of the songs and disgrace the family. She became so anxious that she stopped eating and didn't sleep well. Finally, on the day of the dress rehearsal, the girl really messed up some of her songs. But the director said not to worry, that's what dress rehearsals were all about. Afterwards, however, her father bawled her out for her poor performance. The girl broke down and wept. Then her mother told her she would never be a great actress if she cried when she was criticized. The girl became hysterical and by the time she got home she had a temperature of 102 and had to be put to bed. The next day another girl acting as her understudy had to take her part with only a matter of hours preparation and she did it well.

In the gospel Jesus tells a parable about banquet guests vying for the places of honor. The advice he gives may seem at first to be a little cynical. We wonder why Jesus would bother. What difference does it make whether you get the first place at the banquet or not? Maybe the strategy Jesus suggests is a good one; maybe if you come in and sit at the lowest possible position and you are somebody famous, then you look really good when the person throwing the banquet spots you and brings you up to the front to sit at the main table. But didn't Jesus have better things to do than teach his followers the tricks of the banquet circuit?

Obviously, Jesus is using a story about protocol and etiquette to teach us something else. The shrewd banquet-goer, knowing exactly who he is and what he is worth, will take his place a little bit lower than that to which he is entitled, so that it looks to others like he is being promoted. The shrewd Christian, says Jesus, knows his own strengths and weaknesses and doesn't pretend to be better (or worse) than he is. Whatever good we do we do because God has given us the life and strength to do it; whatever bad we do can never be so bad as to cause us to lose God's love. We are sinners who have been forgiven, sinners who will continue to need forgiveness, and because of God's love, continue to receive it. This is truth, this is shrewd self-evaluation, and this is humility.

Humility is often taken to mean the denial of one's talent. (I really didn't deserve to score 95 on my test; I was just lucky. Or I didn't really throw in those 40 points; the other guys just passed to me a lot and I was lucky. I'm not really gorgeous; I've just learned how to use makeup. I really didn't have such a good year; a couple of things just fell my way and I made a few extra dollars.) Self-deprecation might be a shrewd tactic to fend off envy but it should not be confused with humility. Those who deprecate their own achievements and talents should not believe their own self-deprecation.

151

Don't pretend you're not good when you are—at least don't pretend to yourself.

And don't assume that some special talent, ability, attractiveness, or success makes you worth more than other human beings. For in basic human dignity the millionaire and the pauper have exactly the same worth, though one may have more clout than the other. The pauper who thinks that humility means acknowledging the millionaire's superiority is simply wrong. The millionaire is superior in only one dimension of human achievement and may very well be inferior to the pauper in other dimensions (though not necessarily so). Humility is not a relative matter. In its essence it does not consist of making comparisons with others or of pretending (to yourself or to others) that you are someone different than who you are. The virtue of humility throws away measuring tapes and yardsticks, calculators and computers; it does not ask who am I relative to someone else. Do I make as much money as they do? Do I get the grades they do? Do I make more baskets than they do? Humility has to do with honest self-examination. And in such honest self-regard we perceive that we combine in one person the heights that we are loved by God and the depths that we sin. Because we sin there are no grounds for presumption, and because we are loved by God there is no use for despair. When people ridicule and make fun of us they do not detract one bit from God's love for us; when they praise us and celebrate us for our success, they do not detract one bit from the fact that we are still sinners.

The eighth-grade girl in our opening story was driven to sickness because her parents forgot that her lovability had nothing to do with dramatic success. Even if she was brilliant in her play, it would not make her a better girl. And if she had failed, she would not have been worse. Humility would have helped them (and her) to understand that while it is nice to succeed and it is disconcerting to fail, success does not make the actor any more of a saint or a sinner, or anything less than someone who is deeply loved by God and whose sins will be forgiven by God. (Even eighth-grade girls sin sometimes.) This does not mean, of course, that our imaginary heroine should not want to do well, should not practice hard and should not try to be the best she possibly can. It is paradoxically true that people are often good at precisely those things on which their whole identity does not depend and they are likely to mess up those things on which it does. Our real identity is that of a beloved sinner, and once we accept that, we are free to do well the other things in our life.

(Luke 14:1,7-14)

Standing by your friends

A CERTAIN man was running for mayor of a great city. He had grown up in a neighborhood of the city, worked in summer jobs for the city government, went to law school with financial help from one of the local politicians, and became part of the regular party organization. Then, finally, after a successful career as a lawyer, he decided to run for mayor; and the organization supported him enthusiastically, with precinct captains and the ward committeemen working doggedly to get out the votes and to raise the funds for his campaign. He won a narrow victory only because of the hard work of the politicians out in the precincts. Then, after he was elected, he appointed to positions of power and importance reformers and volunteers and independents and college professors, and rewarded none of the party faithful who had done the hard work. "You need me," he told the faithful, "more than I need you." Then, four years later, when he decided to run for reelection, the reformers, volunteers, independents, and college professors nominated their own candidate. The mayor went to the chairman of the county organization and asked the organization for support. "Hey," said the chairman, "where were you when we needed you?"

If Jesus were telling the parable with which we began, his conclusion might have been, "You can be a 'reformer' or a 'regular,' but you can't be both. You can follow me or you can follow the wisdom of this world, but you can't do both." Jesus would no more be giving advice on how one should vote in an election than on how one should regulate relationships with one's family.

The point of Jesus' advice to renounce our family and possessions is not how we should regulate relationships with our relatives but how we should determine what is important in life. Jesus tells us that the vision of our heavenly Father's love, which he has come to preach, is what really counts. Everything else is important only if it fits in with responding to the heavenly Father's love. While one should not turn against one's family, obviously, save in those circumstances in which the family becomes a serious barrier to religious belief and practice, the message of the gospel is not merely limited to that perhaps rather unusual situation.

What must never be forgotten is the unimportance of everything else compared to standing by Jesus. In politics you stand by your friends. A great politican once said, "If you don't stand by your friends, who will you stand by?" Another remarked, "Someone who is not loyal to his friends, will never be loyal to an idea." Jesus is, in effect, telling us in today's gospel, "Hey, I am your closest friend, your strongest ally, your most powerful supporter, your most enthusiastic admirer. If you don't stand by me, you are not loyal to me. Whom will you stand by, whom will you be loyal to? And whom can you expect to be loyal to you and to stand by you?" The gospel message then, is about loyalty. Jesus has made an unreserved and total commitment of loyalty to us, and he expects the same kind of loyalty in return—not as a matter of political tradeoff but as a matter of an essential dimension in his relationship with us. In the absence of our loyalty to him, there are no channels through which his grace can come to our assistance. Jesus needs our loyalty, in other words, because without it, he cannot provide us with the strength and the vigor and the enthusiasm we need to live a happy, responsive, responsible, generous, unselfish life.

We know that this is true in our relationships. When we cut ourselves off from others, it becomes almost physically impossible for them to help us. In the story with which we began, even the chairman of the regular organization could not persuade his precinct captains and his ward committeemen to work for a candidate who had betrayed them once. No matter how hard they tried, their hearts simply would not be in it. Having cut them off from himself, the mayor also cut himself off from them. With the best will in the world they could not break through the barriers that he had erected. Similarly with Jesus, if we do not make loyalty to his gospel one of the primary goals and purposes in our life, then we have built barriers that will make it difficult—though never impossible—for his grace to crack through our indifference, our hostility, our selfishness, our pettiness. Few of us will turn against Jesus as explicitly as the mayor turned against his supporters in our story. But many of us lead lives of religious routine and indifference by pretending that our days are not numbered, that we can eat our cake and have it too, that we can build up security through our possessions, pleasures and powers, and that we are something other than totally and completely dependent on God's power and love.

(Luke 14:25-33)

Learning to love one another

ONCE there was a woman who was the best real estate agent in her part of the country. She was so good at it that she made more money in her part-time job than her husband, who was a noted lawyer, made in his full-time job. It didn't bother him at all. Jokingly, he said he looked forward to her making so much money that he wouldn't have to work ever again. And her children were proud of her too because she was number one and the kids used to cheer for her every time she sold a house. The secret of her success was that she was unfailingly pleasant, patient and genuinely interested in her clients. She even admitted that she would sell real estate for nothing because she enjoyed meeting new people so much. But after a while it seemed she was interested only in her clients and sensitive only to them. She didn't have time to hear about her husband's cases or to go to her children's basketball games and plays. She became very touchy and impatient with them. Finally, her oldest daughter said to her, "Hey, mom, you've become like bad news. How can you act so charming with your clients but like a total nerd with us?" Stunned, the woman took some time off, even made a retreat, and began working on changing her behavior.

Our story above has to do with a woman who is sensitive, sympathetic and patient to those whom she merely likes and is insensitive, impatient and unsympathetic to those whom she really loves, not because careerwomen are any more likely to do this than careermen (they are probably less likely in fact because on the whole women are more patient, sensitive and sympathetic than men); but it seems proper that in the contemporary world at least some of our stories dealing with occupation and profession be about women as well as about men. When the woman in our story came home from her retreat she said to her daughter, "I wouldn't put up with your father if he had tried to do what I was doing." "Fer shur," said her daughter.

The peculiar behavior of the astute but dishonest steward about whom Jesus talks in the gospel is something in which all humans engage: we let the important things interfere with the essential. We are shrewd, attentive, careful, persistent, determined, agile, and even, if needs be, ruthless in pursuing the important goals of business and profession and lazy and indifferent at pursuing the essential goals of interpersonal intimacy and love both with our families and with God. We will talk for hours and days on end, go to meetings all over the country, constantly update our occupational skills, and simply not discuss the problems of our marriage or family life, much less spend any time at all thinking and discussing our spiritual life. We will admit, of course, that the intimate aspects of our life are absolutely essential, but when you are obsessed with the important you don't have much time for the essential. In the gospel Jesus is in effect telling us that when we are dealing with the essential things we should follow the same kind of strategy that is second nature to us when we are working on that which is important.

The difficulty with the essential is that it can be postponed—or so it seems—whereas the important cannot be postponed. Finishing a product, performing an operation, preparing for a trial, selling real estate, publishing a book, correcting exams—all are things that have to be done right now. The love of a husband and wife, the problems of a child, the invitation of God to respond to his love can be postponed. If we don't take care of them today, there's always tomorrow or the next day. Isn't there? And there always is, at least until the day after the last day of our life. And then there isn't tomorrow or the next day. But in a way that is hardly the point. If we postpone the essential in order to do the important, then we are only half human; we live lives in which we respond to the demands of the world outside of us, and never impose our own personality, our own goodness, our own talent, our own skill, our own affection, our own love on the world. Okay, God may be merciful and give us the time at the end of our life to straighten out things with him and with those we love; or he may love us so much that he will forgive us even if we don't manage to sneak in that last day or week or month for reconciliation. But what wonderful opportunities have been wasted, and what will one feel like at the end of life if one can look back on six, seven, or even eight decades in which one has done all the important things and not done any (or done badly) the essential things?

From time to time, let us pause, take stock, examine our lives, and see what we have done so far. Let us ask ourselves whether we have permitted the important to sweep away the essential, whether we have continued to be extremely clever, crafty, and shrewd about the important things and utterly indifferent, stupid, insensitive, and improvident when it comes to the essential things. Have we been cheating on our most intimate loves? Have we been cheating God becuase of the deadline we have to meet tomorrow, or because of next week's schedule, or because of this quarter's program? It would not make a nice epitaph, would it: "He (she) did the important well but found no time for the essential."

(Luke 16:1-13)

Our ingratitude to God

ONCE upon a time, way into the future, in a galaxy that's not too far from us, there was an emperor called Finnbar the Fair. He was the Emperor of All the World and Everything Else Besides, and he was also the Greatest Wizard in All the World and Everything Else Besides. He was also a seventeen-year-old combination of Luke Skywalker and John Denver. Anyway, there was this town in his empire that was being besieged by an armada of trolls, an army of flying dragons, and several infantry divisions of ogres. The town was in deep trouble. Its food supply was almost exhausted, its water was low, it was running out of ammunition, and the morale of the garrison had reached rock bottom. Emperor Finnbar heard about all this and was upset. So he took his horse, Silver, and his girlfriend, Deirdre the Dark, and rode to the town one night. They slipped through the enemy lines and informed the garrison that there was nothing more to worry about because Finnbar the Fair was in charge. He cast a few minor spells (white magic, of course, because he was a good wizard), sprinkled around a few potions, and murmured a few incantations. Poof! The trolls, the dragons and the ogres disappeared; the supermarkets in town filled up with food, the water in the reservoir lapped against the high edge, and the townsfolk sang and danced and celebrated. "Aren't you forgetting something?" said Finnbar the Fair, leaning forward expectantly on the great white horse Silver. "I've never seen it to fail," he muttered to Deirdre the Dark. "You drive away the demons and evil spirits and nobody even bothers to say 'thank you.' It just goes to show. . . ."

Finnbar the Fair is a silly character in a silly story. But ingratitude is silly too. The people who are too busy, too proud, too arrogant, or too thoughtless to say "thanks" are foolish, ridiculous, absurd, comic people. Good is done to them and they accept the good not as pure gift but as something to which they have an absolute right. For only if you have an absolute right to good are you in a position not to say "thanks." The nine lepers who did not return to give gratitude to Jesus acted as though the cure was theirs as a matter of right. Jesus had no claim on their gratitude. Oh, we might excuse them with the argument that they were so thrilled, so surprised, so happy, and so eager to tell their families about the gift of health that they forgot gratitude. But to forget something so important is to deny the giftedness of the gift and to act as if you had a right to it.

Parents are always insistent that little children learn to say thank you when something is given to them. They are humiliated when children forget to say it, and they become furious when teenagers—in their sullen phases—maintain that it is demeaning and humiliating to thank anyone. Yet those same parents forget to thank one another. In fact, years can go by in marriage in which gratitude becomes as vestigial as one's appendix. We are profoundly offended when someone doesn't thank us but as thoughtless as the nine lepers when it is our turn to express gratitude.

And, if we are honest about it, we will admit that some of the human resistance to saying "thank you" comes from pride and arrogance. We don't want to be dependent on others; we don't want to be vulnerable toward them. Sincere graditude is an act of both dependence and vulnerability, admittedly an act which makes us more rather than less appealing, but if appeal means vulnerability, many, indeed most, of us would sooner not be appealing.

Gratitude to God for the gifts he has given us and gratitude to our fellow humans correlate. The person who remembers to say thank you to God will also remember to say thank you to human benefactors, and the one who has no time for gratitude to those humans who give him gifts will also have no time to thank God. Our relationships with God, and especially our prayer relationships, are mirror images of our human relationships. Gratitude in one affects gratitude in the other and vice versa. For most of us, it is much to be feared, the words "thank God" are either a meaningless exclamation or an occasional prayer when something wonderful or special happens in our life or when some terrible harm is averted. They are not a habitual and characteristic part of our religious life any more than they are typical and characteristic of our relational lives. We are very good at praying to God for things (and there is nothing wrong with that); we are not so good at being grateful afterwards, and surely not very good at expressing general gratitude for our life, the food we eat, the water we drink, the air we breathe, the family who loves us, and the friends who stand by us. Indeed, God has given us so much that we could spend all our time in prayers of gratitude; but it is still not an adequate response. It is impossible to be excessive in prayers of gratitude.

The excuse for ingratitude, in our relationships both with other people and with God, is thoughtlessness, heedlessness. Nobody turns out deliberately to be ungrateful (though sometimes our unconscious needs drive us to punish the giver, in line with the adage "No good deed goes unpunished"). Our ingratitude, like so many other unappealing dimensions of our personalities, is a result of distraction, inattention, confusion, the insistent demands of the monotony and routine of our daily life. The lepers probably had a lot of things to "catch up on," and they intended to thank Jesus "when they got around to it." Only they never got around to it. The inhabitants of the town probably had every intention of thanking Finnbar the Fair, but after all, there was so much work to do after a seige that they never quite got around to it. Gratitude to God and gratitude to our fellow human beings get swept away and filed permanently in a cabinet labeled "to be done when I get around to it." Of course, at the end of our lives that file is enormous.

(Luke 17:11-19)

Who said marriage was easy?

PICTURE a husband and wife who loved one another but who never completely enjoyed their marriage together because they fought too much. Or rather they fought the wrong way. They didn't know how to use the conflict to straighten out their difficulties and facilitate their growth in love. They fought, not to clear the air, but to punish one another. And while they didn't destroy their love, they didn't enjoy it very much. They died suddenly in an auto accident and awoke to find themselves in a pleasant place. They had a comfortable house, a well-stocked refrigerator and bar, a tennis court, swimming pool—all the comforts they could have imagined. "Maybe we're in heaven," said the wife. "But if we're in heaven," said the husband, "where is everybody else?" They went swimming, played tennis, barbecued some steaks, watched television, and had a rip-roaring argument. And the next day they did the same thing. They did try once to get outside of the wall around the house, but found all the doors were locked. They just couldn't get out. "This is much too pleasant to be hell," said the wife. "But if it's heaven, where is everybody else?"

Then God appeared on the tennis court. "Do you like it here?" God asked. "Sure," said the husband, "but where are we? It's not hell, is it?" "Of course not," said God. "But it's not heaven either," said the wife. "If it were," God said, "you wouldn't have fought last night. And you'll probably fight today, too. Indeed, you'll probably fight here forever unless you both change."

"Purgatory!" said the husband and wife together. "Right," replied God. "For you two, Purgatory will consist of being cut off from everybody but yourselves, and I will only let you out of here when you make up for all the time you wasted in life and learn how to love one another."

"We can't fight in heaven?" asked the wife dubiously.

"Sure, there's diagreement in heaven," said God. "But in heaven when people disagree they don't hurt one another. Now go on and play tennis, but realize that if you argue over tennis you're just prolonging your time in Purgatory."

In the gospel Jesus responds to those who have an excessively contractual and proprietary approach to marriage, emphasizing that in heaven love has nothing to do with the transmission of family property. He does not say there is no love in heaven. Especially he does not say husbands and wives won't love one another in heaven. Quite the contrary. The intimacy between husbands and wives will be even greater in heaven than it is here on earth, though we have no idea what that intimacy will be like, save that it will be more rewarding than here on earth. Jesus is less interested in describing what heaven will be like than he is in criticizing a fallacious view of marriage, the view that marriage was essentially a family arrangement for passing on property. He tells his audience that that may be the way in which people live in marriage here on earth, but love in heaven will have nothing to do with family property.

Rarely in our time are there such things as arranged marriages and dividing up and passing on of family property at the time of marriage. So the gospel story does not have this implication for us. The basic message, however, is as important today as it was then: marriage is an intimate relationship between two people in which they must learn how to love one another in order that they might be able to love God. It isn't an easy relationship. Even in the happiest marriages, love demands patience and sensitivity, and sympathy and generosity and hard work. But the idea of our modern story is surely reasonable. Either we learn to love God by learning to love one another in this life, or somehow we are going to have to learn the meaning of unselfish love somewhere else before we are ready to cope directly with God. Purgatory for fiction writers is often perceived as a place where we straighten out the messes we have made in our relationships as a preparation for final and ultimate happiness. Will purgatory really be a place where husbands and wives have to straighten out the mess they have made of their marriage relationships? We can't say for sure, and the church doesn't say anything official on the subject, but wouldn't it be poetic justice? Wouldn't purgatory be an appropriate place for you husbands and you wives to straighten out the kinks in your relationship? As we have God saying to the couple in our opening image, "No mixed doubles for you two until you learn how to stop hurting one another."

There are enormous rewards in marital love—physical, psychological, emotional, spiritual. And there are also enormous fears that stand in the way of that love. We come together in our human intimacies with a baggage of bad habits, insecurities, defense mechanisms, twisted response patterns, dislikes of members of the opposite sex, and neat little tricks for punishing those whom we love—many of which we have learned from our own parents. So despite the attraction of man and woman for one another and despite the enormous rewards that come from that attraction, it is very easy to mess up our intimacies badly and sometimes irretrievably. Men play the macho, order-giving, dominating, aggressive hero; and women play the sly, subtle, downputting, ego-destroying know-it-all. These are patterns of relationship that both have learned and which are deeply structured in our society. Okay, God says in effect, act that way if you want, but don't think you are going to get away with it. I call to you for generous love, a love that leaves behind the stereotypical. Learn to love me through your beloved now, for it's going to be much harder later on.

There are arguments, fights, explosions in all close relationships. The issue is not whether we can avoid or eliminate our conflicts, but can we learn how to turn them into situations that help us to mature in our own selfhood and in the generosity of our love toward others. In a marriage where these skills have been acquired, however painfully, the husband and wife are indeed lessening their purgatory here on earth. In those marriages where these skills haven't been learned, there is a lot of purgatory still ahead.

(Luke 20:27-38)

Resisting temptation

A YOUNG lawyer working for a government investigation agency stumbled on to some evidence that a certain very powerful politician was guilty of a serious crime. The evidence he found was such that if he destroyed it no one would ever know. If he turned the evidence over to his superiors, the politician would certainly be indicted, convicted, and perhaps even sent to jail. The politician suspected that the young man had found the particular piece of evidence and sent word to him that if he destroyed it and said nothing about it, that politician would guarantee him $100,000 in cash, tax free, every year for the rest of his life. Moreover, he would guarantee the young man a successful political career. "You don't even have to destroy the evidence," was the message. "Hang onto it if you want so that you can be certain I'll live up to my promises. And don't think your superiors will thank you for forcing them to confront and indict such an important person as myself. Even if you were to win the case—and you may not—such a victory won't guarantee you promotion or success. Take my money, don't ruin my life, and nobody will be hurt." For a solid week the young man agonized over the decision and finally decided that his oath of office was more important than money and success. He turned the evidence over to a grand jury.

For our purposes in this meditation the important point is *not* that the young man made the right decision. The important thing is that he hesitated and wrestled with the temptation, almost giving in to it. Indeed some nights he went to bed having decided he would give in to it, only to change his mind the next morning. But didn't the young man actually commit a sin when he failed to refuse the politician's offer immediately? And didn't he make the sin worse when he permitted himself to fall asleep having decided to accept the bribe? Instead of admiring the courage of his final decision, should we not disapprove of his hesitation?

What matters about temptation is not how long it lasts, not how seductive it is, but whether we finally give in to it either by actually doing what the temptation invites us to do or by making up our mind that we would do it if we could do so. The length, the attractiveness, the frequency, the intensity of the temptation do not move the temptation one inch toward sin. If this young man had indeed gone along with the bribe offer, he probably would have done so by default. He would have decided not to decide and in that process, he would have accepted the money and torn up the evidence without ever admitting to anyone that he had made the morally wrong decision. Temptations are rejected decisively, but some are succumbed to by indifference and drift. When we succumb to temptation we don't quite explicitly say yes. Rather, we say no with progressively less vigor. The yes becomes our de facto answer. The check is deposited and the evidence destroyed as if someone else were doing it.

There are many temptations in our daily lives that parallel the temptations of Jesus. For example, we are often tempted to take out our frustrations on those who are not able to defend themselves against us. Our children and our spouse, for example, are likely to become the targets of our anger and our cruelty when we cannot express the anger we feel toward our work associates. We use those who are subordinate to us, in our work or familial environment, as tools to enhance our own ego, our own self-importance, our own feelings of domination and power. We permit ambition and greed for acclaim to become the overriding concern in our lives so that no one, no matter how intimate or how important, is permitted to be an obstacle in our climb to power. Moreover, these temptations to use others for power, pleasure, acclaim, and wealth can even be justified by the self-deceiving argument that what we are doing to them is something they have brought upon themselves or is for their own good or is an exercise of our basic rights and responsibilities.

The temptations of Jesus are reported to us as evidence of his humanity. Jesus was not merely an actor playing a part, but someone sharing humanity with the rest of us, and therefore someone who understood the meaning of the temptation experience. But the worst thing we can do with the temptation story is to reduce it to a play-acting scenario. The temptations in the life of Jesus are every bit as real as those we experience. The strategy with which Jesus dealt with them is as necessary for us as it was for him. He said the firm and decisive "no" more quickly and more firmly than most of us could, perhaps, but still it was the no we must say to all the temptations, big and little, in our life. And as we well know, the little ones are as important in their way as the big ones.

If the man in our opening story had made a habit of accepting small gifts, fixing traffic tickets, cheating a bit on his income tax, closing his eyes to minor abuses that he was supposed to uncover, then he would have developed habits and attitudes that would have made it much easier to say a de facto yes to what might have been the biggest temptation in his life. Jesus resisted the temptations to infidelity—to be unfaithful to the mission the heavenly Father had given him—because during his life he had developed through practice the virtue of fidelity. The scripture saying that he who is faithful in small things will be faithful in big things is not only good religion, it is sound psychology.

(Matthew 4:1-11)

The ultimate bad news

"YOUR days are numbered!"

Individuals who have been on the receiving end of such devastating news have provided the subject matter for hundreds of stories, novels and plays down through the years. The sympathies and emotions aroused are so powerful that an author or dramatist who uses any variation of the theme has little trouble engaging the interest of an audience. So much so that the "death sentence" as a dramatic device has become something of a cliche—a "cheap shot"—which can usually be discovered during almost any week of televised soap-opera serials.

Familiarity, as another cliche goes, usually breeds contempt but, in this instance, no matter how many times and in how many ways we have encountered it in the lives and stories of others, none of us are really prepared to hear such terminal news about ourselves, or those we love. Even though we read stories of saints and fictional characters who, through prayer and strength of character, have transcended their feelings of terror and present a brave face to the world, we have no confidence that we would be able to do the same. One thinks of Thomas More's brave humor in the face of death—accepting a helping hand to mount the steps of the scaffold and announcing that he would need no help coming down them and asking the executioner to spare his beard when he wielded his axe since it had in no way offended King Henry VIII. Or of Sidney Carton in Dickens' novel *A Tale of Two Cities*, who, having

173

managed to save the life of another by substituting himself on the list of those to die at the guillotine, proclaims nobly that it is a far, far nobler thing that he is doing by dying than he has ever done before.

But who knows what fear really stalked their hearts. Even Jesus, during his agony in the garden, was human enough to pray that if the Father's will could be accomplished in another way, that he be spared the passion and death he saw before him.

It is difficult for us to accept the fact that Jesus himself did not know that the coming of the Kingdom which he preached did not entail the destruction and end of the world in the immediate future but he did insist that the coming of the Kingdom was close at hand and admits (in Matthew 13:32-37) that "As to the exact day or hour, no one knows, neither the angels in heaven nor even the Son, but only the Father." We do know that Paul and the early believers did expect the end of the world and the Parousia to overtake them at any hour. This means that they believed their days on earth were numbered and Paul gave them explicit instructions on how to go about living out these last days on earth: "Those who have wives should live as though they had none (abstain from sex and procreation); those who mourn should live as if they had nothing to mourn for (there's no point since all will be reunited soon in the Kingdom); those who are enjoying life should live as if there were nothing to laugh about (the coming of the Lord is a serious and profound time); those whose life is buying things should live as though they had nothing of their own (you can't take it with you and, in any case, material wealth is antithetical to the Kingdom); and those who have to deal with the world should not become engrossed in it (the world will be gone, time is better spent preparing and repenting).

This did not necessarily mean that the early Christians expected to die, but rather that they expected to witness these things, be part of them and be transformed to another life. They expected this to be frightening, or at least awe-inspiring, but also a certain justification of their faith and sacrifice.

This passionate conviction in both the imminent end of the world and the Second Coming which the Apostles preached so eloquently after Pentecost and which Paul carried everywhere in his travels was evidently so compelling that it went a long way toward accounting for the phenomenal growth of Christianity, right from its inception. These men and women were so obviously convinced and so radically preparing themselves for "the end of the world as we know it" that their words of repentance and hope in risen Jesus made enormous impact—impact capable of converting whole families and even cities—a fervor which the reading from the book of Jonah fortells in the account of the saving of the entire great city of Nineveh from God's wrath. As more and more time passed, however, it was only natural that the ardor of these new converts may have begun to cool—people died as before, life went on as before.

Paul wrote to remind everyone that just because it had not happened did not mean it would not happen and that they were to continue to live accordingly. As for those who died before having the chance to be witness to the Second Coming, Paul assured them that all would return with the triumphant risen Jesus.

Almost two thousand years later we are still waiting for "the end of the world as we know it"—though our world would probably seem more than sufficiently different to Paul to have already fulfilled his prophecy. We have, of course, long since abandoned his specific instructions to the Corinthians as to how to live in the "end time." The world is thoroughly engrossed in itself, does business, laughs, mourns and procreates. Does this mean that the Second Coming is pointless nonsense? Of course not. We would do well to heed Paul's tacit warning that just because it has not happened yet does not mean that it is never going to happen. As a matter of fact, looking at the all-too-menacing tensions in the world, and considering the terrible nuclear potential to destroy ourselves by pressing a few red buttoms, we have far better reason to expect instant apocalypse than did the early Christians, even more reason to repent and live as if the Kingdom were about to overtake us.

But these are universal considerations. What of those who learn, as so many of us do today, that cancer or some other fatal affliction has numbered our days? The evolution of modern medical science has dramatically increased the numbers who get this message with clinical certainty. There are all too many who know with certainty that their hour will come next week, or next month or, in any case, before their appointed hour. What they, and all of us whose days are numbered, must come to accept is that life is a mystery, a gift freely given; that it comes with no factory guarantee of longevity; but also that God, through his Son, with whom we can claim kinship, offers still another gift of prodigal generosity—a place in his Kingdom which is suddenly, actually at hand.

(1 Corinthians 7:29-31)

A challenging invitation

BRENDAN is a student at a prestigious university. He's a very good, sound, diligent, and devout young man. He also has a few problems. Until recently, he didn't study very much. He tends to go out a lot at night with the guys and on some nights, heaven save us all, he even drinks a little bit more beer than he ought to drink. You will observe that Brendan is probably the first male college student in history to be afflicted by such faults!

So anyway, during a lunch hour not so long ago, Brendan was in the student union cafeteria desperately cramming—that afternoon he had two tests, an interview with his adviser, and a paper to finish for yet another course. Poor Brendan was also dangerously close to academic probation and, if the truth be told, only a hop, skip, and a jump away from flunking out of college. His mother and father had had stern words with him on the phone the night before, telling him he simply had to shape up and settle down and act like an adult—instructions they had been giving him since he was nine. Brendan, who was a good-hearted soul, agreed with his parents (as he had agreed with them since he was nine). He resolved once more, but this time very seriously, that he was going to shape up, settle down, study and get the A's to which his intelligence entitled him, make the Dean's list, give a good example to his younger brothers and sisters, and take a big load of worry off his parents' minds.

So there was Brendan, eating a healthy lunch—guacamole yogurt, french fries, and Diet Coke—when

178

he heard someone walking up to his table. I have no time to talk to anybody, he said to himself. I've got to study for my two exams and finish my term paper and get ready for my conference with my advisor. I won't even look up. "Are you saving this place?" said a young female voice.

"No, I'm not," Brendan said, without looking up. Ah, a stalwart young man was our hero Brendan.

"May I sit down?"

Brendan thought to himself that they usually didn't ask. "It's a free country." He then sneaked a peak out at the farthest corner of his left eye. It was The Girl.

Brendan didn't know her name, but he spent half of his time in English Literature 202 staring at her. She wasn't *exactly* the kind of person who would appear in the swimsuit ads in *Sports Illustrated*, but she was GORGEOUS—black hair, pale white skin, big blue eyes, tall, slender, with just a touch of mystery about her.

"Studying for the tests?" she asked, digging into her container of chili-cheese yogurt.

"Uh huh," Brendan muttered, sternly sticking to his resolution.

"Do you like English Literature 202?" She munched on her french fries.

"Can't you see I'm studying?" Brendan actually snarled at The Girl.

"Sorry," she sort of giggled.

Brendan stuck to his studying, and the young woman stuck to eating her yogurt. Every once in a while, however, Brendan would peek up out of that same corner of his left eye and notice that she was sitting there across the table, sort of smiling at him, like she was amused and not angry. She's looking at me the way I think I look at her in class, Brendan thought.

Could it be, said a voice (a demon or an angel is irrelevant to our story) in the far corner of his brain, that this is not only The Girl but The One. If you talk to her, might the rest of your life not be different and much better? You're not going to learn anything studying now that you wouldn't learn anyway, and maybe if you're just a little friendly, she might even agree to go out with you in six months or so.

No way, Brendan murmured to himself. I have to study.

So, he crammed more facts and more numbers and more dates and places and names into his head and didn't look up at all anymore, except maybe once every minute. Because The Girl was like totally beautiful.

Finally, she finished her chili-cheese yogurt and stood up. "Good luck on the test, Brendan," she said.

Wasn't that just like a girl to know his name when he didn't know hers?

"Mmmm."

"Don't forget to finish your guacamole yogurt," and she walked away.

Brendan followed her with his eyes as she slipped through the student union cafeteria and out the doors. She was indeed like totally gorgeous.

You're an idiot, Brendan told himself. The Girl was inviting you to become a friend. She may even like you just a little bit, and despite what everybody else says, she seems to think you're not a total geek. That was the opportunity of a lifetime she was offering you and you blew it. Brendan, you're an idiot, a ninny, a nerd and a jerk.

In The Gospel, we read of Jesus inviting men and women to come after him. It is an extremely attractive invitation because Jesus is an extremely attractive person, but we are warned that if we do follow after him, we'll have to make sacrifices and we may even have to suffer, but we will also be rewarded. The point in the gospel story is not that we should be disloyal to our family and our friends. The point is rather that we should permit nothing to interfere with our following after Jesus. It is an opportunity of a lifetime. An exciting, wondrous, marvelous challenge. We ought to concentrate not on the sacrifices we'll have to make, not on the difficulties that are going to be involved, not on the strains and tensions that following in the footsteps of Jesus might create; but rather on the opportunity, the excitement, the wonder, and the challenge.

The opening story about Brendan, who in a fit of frantic virtue turned down an invitation from The Girl, parallels precisely the story in the Gospel. Brendan geeked out for perfectly fine and wonderful reasons. He had two tests, he had to finish a term paper, he had an appointment with his adviser, and his parents were angry with him again. So he didn't have time for The Girl. (Her real name, by the way, was Sheilaigh, but that gets ahead of our story too.) He had a marvelous excuse for being rude to the most beautiful, the most mysterious, the most wonderful girl he had ever seen in all his life. Brendan blew it. He blew it with the best possible of excuses, but still he blew it.

Thus, with us. We are invited each day to come follow Jesus; to live lives of responsiveness, openness, generosity, love. And we decline the invitation with the best possible reasons—our obligations, our responsibilities, our commitments, our crucial concerns, our schedules, our deadlines, our families, our friends—all perfectly splendid reasons. But the truth of the matter is that we are just a little bit afraid of the roller coaster ride that results when we come follow Jesus. Just as, if the truth be told, Brendan not only adored The Girl, but was also frightened by her.

There are three conclusions we can draw from our parable of Brendan and The Girl:

First, the invitation to follow Jesus is much like The Girl's invitation to Brendan—attractive, mysterious, enticing, a little bit scary, and promising great adventure, hard work, and much challenge.

Second, Jesus calls us to come follow after him precisely in and through the important people that offer us invitations in our lives. This is what Catholicism means by the principle of sacramentality. Our invitations to follow Jesus come for the most part through those who are closest to us, most important to us, who care for us the most, and whom we love the most. There is a very strong possibility—but that gets us ahead of the story again, doesn't it—that The Girl would have been a real sacrament for Brendan. Enthralled by her wit, charm, and intelligence, he really might have settled down and shaped up, because it would have been even more important to please her than to please his parents. God's grace may have been sitting across the table from Brendan during that lunch hour, eating chili-cheese yogurt. So our story is not only a parable, it is also a sacrament.

Third, come on now, do you really think that The Girl (whose name is Sheilaigh, but you're still not supposed to know that yet) has given up on Brendan just because he geeked out in the student union cafeteria? If she was that easily discouraged, then she certainly wouldn't have been The Girl. And, of course, we know that she was. Poor Brendan. He's really not going to get away from her at all. She'll keep trying until he finally decides that keeping her happy is the most important thing in his life, and then you just wait until Brendan settles down and shapes up and gets on the Dean's list! Like The Girl, God doesn't give up either. He is, after all, the hound of heaven who relentlessly pursues us down the nights and down the years with unperturbed pace and majestic instancy. Brendan is very likely going to see The Girl at a basketball game that night to which she knows he's going. What do you want to bet she's going to be sitting close to him—not too close, but close enough so that he'll see her? What do you want to bet that's the same way God pursues us? Try as we might, it's very difficult to escape God's passionate love.

(Matthew 10:37-42)